Aspects of ARABIC & Translation of THE QUR'ÂN

ALI AL-HALAWANI

ISBN: 978–9–6715–82008
ISBN-13:

DEDICATION

To the good souls of my late father, mother and elder brother.

CONTENTS

FOREWORD

All praise is due to Allah, and Allah's Peace and Blessings be upon His Final Messenger, his pure family, his noble Companions, and all those who follow them with righteousness until the Day of Judgment.

This book explores a selection of topics related to the Arabic language, the linguistic style of the Qur'ân and its inimitability, and the translation of the meanings of the Qur'ân into English.

No doubt, the Arabic language has been, and still is, one of the most widely spoken languages across the globe. It has deeply rooted itself in human history; its magnificent influence on humankind is undeniable. Around 15 centuries ago, it became the language of Islam: the fastest growing faith in the world today. After that, it came to the fore as the language of scholarship and scientific research in nearly all fields, and many peoples of the world acquired knowledge and sought progress by translating the works written in that very language.

In fact, translation constitutes a bridge of cultural and civilizational communication and understanding among different peoples. It has been and will continue to be so, especially since the world has become a small village where a word or a statement by a politician or a media personality said in the furthermost corner of the globe can affect the opposite corner. Indeed, this can be attributed to the gigantic revolution in the means of communication and the unlimited capabilities it provides. *But, who shoulders this responsibility?* It is the translator who receives the text before anyone else and attempts to transfer its message to the target language(s), thus making it available to the target audience. In so doing, the translator is burdened with a backbreaking mission under which even mountains may collapse if they fully realize its true significance. A mistake may be fatal or enough of a reason to instigate killings. In discussions on the significance of translation, I have often stated, *"Some translations can be killers!"*

A translator is a messenger between cultures. Paz (1914-1998) stated, "Every language is a specific way of viewing and interpreting the world. This is despite the fact that natural phenomena do not change from one country to another. However, it is our way of interacting or tackling these phenomena that significantly differ from one language to another." The translator, then, is the mediator between all these cultures and varied weltanschauungs. He is the one who makes it possible for us to appreciate these worldviews despite the lingual barriers separating us.

Hence, this book is a humble attempt toward shedding more light on the nature of translation with reference to the Qur'ân and the various obstacles the Arabic language, in general, and the language of the Qur'ân, in particular, pose to the translator who attempts to carry out such a great task and noble mission. This book targets two types of audience: firstly, those who are interested in the Arabic language, the language of the Qur'ân, and its translation into foreign languages; secondly, novice and professional translators who shoulder a grave responsibility, namely, contributing to reduce the cultural and civilizational gaps as well as the gap in science between the different people of the world.

It has to be noted here that this book is a highly elaborated and extended version of a published research paper by the author under the title: *Eight-Point Scheme Proposal for Translating the Qur'ânic Text.*[1] But, why did I turn a published research paper into a book? Limitations levied by academia usually make the researcher do without many details when writing research papers which could be very useful and mind-opening. These omitted details along with other related sub-topics convinced me to wholeheartedly accept this laborious task to present to the general reader as well as the professional specialist a relatively detailed work that includes most of the necessary points on the topic at hand.

It is hoped that this book would be accepted and appreciated by the dear reader.

Ali Al-Sayed Al-Halawani

Assistant Professor of Linguistics & Translation Studies, International Islamic University Malaysia (IIUM), Kuala Lumpur, Malaysia.
March, 2018

---

[1] Al-Halawani, *Eight-point scheme proposal for translating the Qur'ânic text,* 91-104.

INTRODUCTION

It is such a pleasure to write an introduction to this valuable book by Dr. Ali Al-Halawani, a distinguished alumnus of the academic institution with which both he and I have been affiliated, namely the Faculty of Languages and Translation, Al-Azhar University, Cairo, Egypt.

Although Dr. Al-Halawani is a prolific author of several publications, which the honourable reader can find listed at the end of the present book, he has decided to publish this treatise online as well so that it may be more easily available to a large audience within the shortest possible time.

The book, which is an enlarged version of a previously published research paper, includes many of the details and various subtopics which the writer had to do without for reasons explained in his Foreword. Thus, in its present form, the book consists of two parts, each of which subsumes several topics that adequately tackle the issues in question.

In Part One, entitled 'Aspects of Arabic', the author concisely, but adequately, discusses such important issues as: Mapping Arabic (in terms of its speakers and different varieties); the unique features of the language of the Noble Qur'ân; why the Qur'ân is inimitable; how the Qur'ân has affected Arabic (in terms of strengthening it, standardizing its tribal dialects, turning it into a universal language, providing a written description of Arabic grammar, and refining Arabic terminology); the features of Arabic and the Arabic script; and finally, the major landmarks in the development of Arabic linguistics.

In Part Two, entitled 'Translation of the Qur'ânic Text', Dr. Al-Halawani discusses in some detail the relation of translation in general to the translation of the Qur'ân in particular, showing that the latter constitutes an attempt at translating the untranslatable. He also discusses the different types of translation with reference to the Qur'ân, viz, literal translation, meaning-based translation, and interpretive translation, side by side with the advantages of the last approach. After that, the author moves on to tackle the problems of translating the Noble Qur'ân, focusing on the common mistakes of translators; then he ends with a discussion of how the Qur'ân should be translated, providing 'golden rules' for achieving this purpose, and finally concludes by shedding some light on some selected translations of the Qur'ân, namely those by Pickthall, Ali, Arberry, Al-Hilali and Khan, and finally Ghali, the founder of the Faculty of Languages and Translation, Al-Azhar University.

Since this second part of the book deals with the issue of translation in general, side by side with the task of rendering the meanings of the Noble Qur'ân into other languages (especially English) in particular, it may be in order to say a brief word about both issues. Basically, there are many definitions of translation, a frequently quoted one being that by Catford, who defined it as "the replacement of textual material in one language (SL) by equivalent textual material in another language (TL)," where SL stands for the source language and TL stands for the target language. At first sight, such a process of replacement may sound easy. Far from it! Translation involves much more than simply mastering both SL and TL. Necessary also, among other things, is a good familiarity with the cultures to which both languages belong.

The difficulty of translating religious texts in general, and the Qur'ân in particular, is enormous, to the extent that even some well-known translators have admitted that it is 'untranslatable', e.g., Pickthall and Ghali. Similarly, Arberry maintained that the Qur'ân's "rhythms and rhymes are inseparable features of the impressive eloquence which are indeed inimitable," whereas Bultemeier holds that the task is "impossible."

I would like to point out that in writing his book Dr. Al-Halawani opted for a clear style and made use of an impressive collection of reference works, including books, journal articles, and internet websites both in English and Arabic, many of which are recent publications–a fact which adds more value to the author's endeavour.

Finally, I beseech Allah (Glorified and Exalted is He) to reward the honourable author for the great effort he exerted in writing his book, and at the same time hope that this academic work will be of benefit to the honourable readers. And our last supplication is: Praise be to Allah, the Lord of the Worlds.

Ahmed Shafik Al-Khatib
    Professor Emeritus,
    Faculty of Languages & Translation,
    Al-Azhar University, Egypt.

ACKNOWLEDGMENTS

All praise is due to Allah, and Allah's Peace and Blessings be upon His Final Messenger, his pure family, his noble Companions, and all those who follow them with righteousness until the Day of Judgment.

I am exceptionally grateful to Dr. Ahmed Shafik Al-Khatib, Professor Emeritus of Linguistics and Translation, Faculty of Languages & Translation, Al-Azhar University, for his precious scholarly notes and editorial remarks on the content of this present book.

My thanks must be registered over and again to my wife, Fatimah Ahmed Ali, for her unremitting help, encouragement and enduring patience and perseverance.

I am also indebted to my editor, publisher and designer for their excellent as well as professional work.

PART ONE

ASPECTS OF ARABIC

1 MAPPING THE ARABIC LANGUAGE

"Any language is human prior to being national: Turkish, French, and German languages first belong to humanity and then to Turkish, French, and German peoples."

Leo Spitzer (1934)

There are 467,000,000 speakers of Arabic worldwide,[2] rendering Arabic as the largest member of the Semitic branch of the Afro-Asiatic language family to which it belongs. It is one of the official languages of the United Nations as well as other international organizations. It has been a written language since the 6th century A.C., and is the liturgical language of Islam.

Arabic, as a term, refers to several varieties of the language, all of which are employed in the Arab world. The

---

[2] Noack & Gamio, *The world's languages,* www.washingtonpost.com.

Arabic-speaking world can best be described as being 'diglossic', as Modern Standard Arabic (MSA) is spoken fluently in the area along with a colloquial variety of Arabic that differs from one region to another. Basically, there are three types of Arabic: Colloquial Arabic, Classical Arabic, and MSA. Furthermore, Al-Sulaiti mentioned a fourth form of Arabic labelled 'Educated Spoken Arabic' (ESA), or the hybrid form.[3]

COLLOQUIAL ARABIC refers to the regional varieties used by Arabs for communication purposes. Colloquial varieties of Arabic are naturally acquired by Arab children as their first language. Numerous spoken dialects vary along geographical, socio-economic, and religious lines. Arabs from one region can usually understand dialects from other regions, depending on their geographical proximity and their command of MSA. There are four major spoken dialects, each of which contains numerous sub-dialects:

Table 1: The four major spoken dialects in the Arab world as adopted by The National Virtual Translation Center (NVTC).[4]

MAGHRIB	EGYPT	LEVANT	GULF
- Morocco - Algeria - Tunisia - Libya - Mauritania	- Sometimes Libya is assigned to this region.	- Syria - Lebanon - Jordan - Palestine - Parts of Iraq	- Saudi Arabia - Yemen - UAE - Oman - Bahrain - Qatar - Kuwait

---

[3] Al-Sulaiti, *Designing and developing a corpus of contemporary Arabic*, 35.

[4] The National Virtual Translation Center (NVTC): www.nvtc.gov.

			- Parts of Iraq

CLASSICAL ARABIC (CA) stands for the Arabic language that has maintained its unique structural and phonetic characteristics throughout the centuries. This is the pure and intact Arabic which is free from any modern styles or terminology. The use of this type of Arabic is now restricted to religious and historical topics, as it does not usually appear in other than classical religious books and manuscripts. Nowadays, one can hear this variety of Arabic only from competent mosque orators and scholars of Islamic studies. Acquiring Classical Arabic can only be achieved through formal instruction at school. It was once the world language of scholarship and religion due to the spread of Islam over most of the globe several centuries ago.

MODERN STANDARD ARABIC (MSA) is the language commonly used in all forms of mass media and authorships. Compared to CA, MSA is much simpler in terms of the terminology and even pronunciation. It is the universal language of the Arab world and a direct descendant of CA. It is used in formal speaking situations such as sermons, lectures, news broadcasts, and speeches, and in all formal writings such as official correspondence, literature and newspapers. There are no native speakers of MSA, as the vast majority of educated Arabs learn this variety of Arabic through formal schooling. On the other hand, it is understandable by most Arab speakers even though they may not have received any formal education in it. It is uniform throughout the Arab world and serves as a *lingua franca* for speakers of various colloquial dialects.

Al-Sulaiti stated there is a fourth form of Arabic referred to in linguistics by the term 'EDUCATED SPOKEN ARABIC' (ESA), *al-lughah al-wusṭa*, or the hybrid form.[5] This

---

[5] Ibid.

form of Arabic derived its features from both the standard and the colloquial varieties of Arabic. Generally, it is used by both educated speakers and by speakers communicating with others from different regions.

Arabs believe, according to Haeri, that their language has been perpetuated and kept alive (only) because it is the language of the Qur'ân.[6] The suitability of Arabic as the language of the Qur'ân is understood by the description of Arabic given by some language experts. For example, Guillaume stated that Arabic "expresses relations with more conciseness than the Aryan languages."[7] This is because of the "extraordinary flexibility" of its verbs and nouns. To him, "Many variations of the fundamental verbal theme can be expressed by vowel changes and consonantal augments" without resorting to any supplementary verbs or pronouns as employed in English, for example. Al-Khalil ibn Aḥmed emphasized this in his book *al-`Ain* (The Eye) as he said, "One should know that a two-letter [Arabic] word can render [in terms of derivation] two different words..., and a three-letter word can render six words..., and a four-letter word can render 24 words..., and a five-letter word can render 120 words".[8]

In a similar vein, some experts in Arabic ascertain that Arabic has more excellence than other languages. They support their saying by citing some reasons, such as those cited by Al-`Alaya'a,[9] which follow:

- Arabic has a perfect pattern of roots which is suited to various and diverse human needs;

- Arabic vocabulary possesses a substantial number of intellectual denotations and connotations.

---

[6] Haeri, *Sacred language, ordinary people.*
[7] Guillaume, *The legacy of Islam*, vi-vii.
[8] Al-Makhzumi & Al-Samiraei, *Al-`Ain* (The eye), 59.
[9] Al-`Alaya'a, *The Arabic language.*

- The system of elementary words in Arabic is perfect. It comprises all noun and verb forms with the same roots and illustrates their mutual relationship as they are arranged in a wise pattern.

- A few Arabic words can convey extensive and exuberant meanings accurately and also precisely.

- Arabic is a perfect means of expressing all subtle human feelings and inner thoughts both precisely and accurately due to its possession of the appropriate roots and idioms needed for the task.

To illustrate this, let us look at an example from *Encyclopedia Britannica;*

"From the root *KTB* 'write', we have *KaTaBna*, 'we wrote', *naKTaBu*, 'we will write', *KaTiBun*, 'writing, a writer', *KiTaBun*, 'a book', *maKTaBun*, 'a place of writing, a school', *muKTiBun* 'a teacher of writing', *taKaTaBa*, 'they two corresponded with one another', *astaKTiBu*, 'I will ask (him) to write', *waKtaTaBa*, 'and he got his name written down (in the register)', *KuTTaBun*, 'scribes', *muKaTaBatun*, 'correspondence', etc." (italics mine).[10]

---

[10] *Encyclopedia Britannica,* www.britannica.com.

2 THE LANGUAGE OF THE QUR'ÂN: ITS UNIQUE FEATURES

*"There is probably in the world no other
book which has remained twelve centuries
with so pure a text."*

Sir William Muir (1819-1905)

The word *'Qur'ân'*, according to Edward Lane, is said to be originally an *inf. n.*; *qara'*, as in *qara't-u al-shaiy'-a* (meaning: 'I collected the thing together'), or as in *qara't-u al-kitab-a* (meaning: 'I read or recited the book or scripture'); and it was then conventionally applied to signify 'The Book of God' that was revealed to Prophet Muḥammad (peace be upon him).[11]

Denffer identified it as "The Word of God (Allah), sent down upon the last Prophet, Moḥammed, through the Angel Gabriel in its precise meaning and precise wording."[12] He

---

[11] Lane, E. W., *An Arabic-English lexicon*, 2504.

[12] Denffer, *Ulum Al-Quran: An introduction to the sciences of the*

explained that Muslims believe that the Qur'ân was then transmitted to us through numerous persons, both verbally and in writing, and that "It is inimitable and unique, protected by Allah from any corruption."[13]

Moreover, the Qur'ân was revealed in the most refined and eloquent of all languages, namely Arabic. According to Ibn Faris, Arabic is believed to be "the most refined of all languages" as it expresses many meanings using very few words. In addition, it is the "most disciplined, organized, eloquent and clear" of all languages. He also stressed that "the language of the Arabs has been divinely-revealed."[14]

Muslims believe that the Qur'ân is Islam's eternal miracle whose inimitability is continually confirmed through scientific research. It is also their belief that it was revealed to Prophet Muhammad (peace be upon him) to bring all men out of the darkness of disbelief and polytheism into the light of faith and monotheism.

Al-Nawawi said in relation to the Qur'ân that any precise objective survey on the number of printed works, research papers, and manuscripts related to the Qur'ân, be it in the past or the present and which amount to tens of thousands, "will decisively prove that the Qur'ân is the only book that ever received so much attention in terms of study, research and in-depth surveys."[15]

Remarkably, Al-Nawawi wrote this nearly 760 years ago. In fact, authoring discourses about the Qur'ân have never ceased, and this book at hand attests to this in a way that needs no further evidence.

Quran, 17.

[13] Ibid.

[14] Ibn Faris, *Al-Sahibi fi Fiqh al-Lughah al-`Arabiyyah.*

[15] Al-Nawawi, *Al-Tibyan fi Adâb Hamalat Al-Qur'ân,* 5.

Distinct Features of the Qur'ânic Language

Purity of the Qur'ânic text has already been acknowledged by many. Muir (1894) wrote, "There is probably in the world no other book which has remained 12 centuries with so pure a text."[16] Similarly, purity of the Qur'ân was stressed by Wherry (2006), who stated, "This text of the Quran is the purest of all the works of alike antiquity."[17]

Dispelling any doubt as to the genuineness of the Qur'ân, Edward Lane (1879) stated that, "There is such an immense amount of merit in the Qur'ân that there is no doubt at all as to its genuineness."[18] He further said that we can now read the Qur'ânic text "with full confidence that it has remained unchanged through nearly thirteen hundred years."[19]

In addition, many Orientalists, none of whom is well-known for his sympathy with Islam and its Prophet, had to acknowledge the fact that the Qur'ân is "the most widely read book in existence."[20]

The Qur'ânic style has a number of unique features that are unshared by any other book ever known to man. Al-Baqillani and Al-Rafi`i cited some of the features that can be summarized as follows:[21]

1. The Qur'ân differs in form from the three modes of expression known to the Arabs at the time of its revelation, namely day-to-day speech, speech of soothsayers, and poetry.

2. Its entire text is free from any discrepancy, as all of its sections enjoy the same standard of rhetoric excellence.

---

[16] Muir, *Life of Mohamet*, vol. 1.

[17] Wherry, *A comprehensive commentary on the Qur'an,* 349.

[18] Lane, E. W., *Selections from the Kur-án,* 16: 3.

[19] Ibid.

[20] See Potter, *The faiths men live by,* 18; Hitti, *History of the Arabs,* 426.

[21] See Al-Baqillani, *I`jâz Al-Qur'ân,* 33-47); Al-Rafi`i, *I`jâz Al-Qur'ân wal-Balaghah al-Nabawiyyah,* 188-208.

No section thereof is better than another. Apparently, this is beyond human capacity as Al-Rafi`i attributed the differences in the styles used by humans to the psychological changes they constantly endure. Were the Qur'ân man-made, its style would inevitably suffer from similar human discrepancies.

3. Unprecedentedly, it originated the terms which express Islamic and *shari`ah*-based meanings and concepts.

Though 'deliberate repetition' was known to the Arabs as a subtle linguistic phenomenon, its occurrence in the Qur'ân confirmed their inability to imitate or produce anything similar to it; even though a particular meaning is expressed in two or three distinct forms therein.

Unlike any terms comprising any other speech, Qur'ânic terms are marked by eloquence and splendour. Generally speaking, if a word were to be replaced in a text by another in the same language, the text would lose an aspect of its originality and eloquence, whatever the similarity between both words may be, as deemed by Al-Lawindi.[22] This is true of any language in general, so how much more for the language of the Qur'ân which is inimitable *per se*? "In its capacity as the Book of Allah," according to Ibn `Attiyah, "If a word was taken out (from its text) and then an exhaustive search was conducted to find a better one to replace it, none would ever be found."[23] Then, what would be the case if the original word was substituted for another from a different language?

Regarding the uniqueness of the Qur'ânic text, Hussein stated, "Linguists have failed to classify the style of the Qur'ân; should it be considered prose or poetry?"[24] According to him, they were bewildered in their attempts to understand

---

[22] Al-Lawindi, *Ishkaliyat Tarjamat Ma`ani Al-Qur'ân Al-Karim*, 22.

[23] See Al-Suyûti, *Al-Muzhir fi `Ulûm al-Lughah wa Anwa`iha*, 308; Musallam, *Mabahith fi I`jaz Al-Qur'ân*, 134-135.

[24] Hussein, *Hadith al-Shi`r wal-Nathr*, 25.

its structures, and finally they considered it "a unique style different from prose and poetry."[25] This is because it is characterized by features uncommon to all other styles. Some of these features are related to the endings of the *ayah*s (verses) and others to its unique musical rhythm, although it is not poetry, because "it does not fall under the [16] known categories of [Arabic] poetry."[26]

Ascertaining the uniqueness of the Qur'ân and the fact that it is incomparable to any similar speech, Al-Jâhiz advocated that different names were given to it and to all its different components to those used in Arabic poetry in a way that proves the dissimilarity between the Qur'ân and poetry, even with regard to actually naming its different components.[27]

---

[25] Ibid.

[26] Ibid.

[27] Al-Suyûṭi, *Al-Muzhir fi `Ulûm al-Lughah wa Anwa`iha*, 1: 178.

3 INIMITABILITY OF THE QUR'ÂN

{Say: Verily, though mankind and the Jinn
should assemble to produce the like of this
Qur'ân, they could not produce the like
thereof though they were helpers one of
another}.

(Qur'ân, Surah Al-Isrâ' 17: 88)

I'jâz al-Qur'ân as a term is translated into English in various ways. Some translators render it as 'inimitable ellipticism', while others use 'miraculous elegance', 'grandiose cadence' or an 'emotive and evocative force'. However, I prefer to use the English equivalent 'inimitability of the Qur'ân' for its simplicity and sufficiency in rendering the term clearly understandable without relying on any awkward structures.

To ascertain the uniqueness of the Qur'ân and the fact that it cannot be compared to any similar speech, different names have been given to it and to all of its components in a way that proves the dissimilarity between the Qur'ân and

Arabic poetry, even with regards to the mere names of the structures. Al-Jâ_hiz_ (159-255 AH) emphasized this by stating that Allah refers to His Book, the Qur'ân, in a way unlike that which the Arabs use to describe their speech, in every aspect. Accordingly, He calls it in its entirety Qur'ân, while they call theirs *diwan* (a collection of poems). He calls one of its 114 parts *surah*, while the Arabs call the unit of their poetry *qa_sîdah* (a poem). He calls a part of one *surah* an *ayah*, while they call theirs' *bâyt* (a line of poetry or verse). He calls the end of each *ayah* a *fâ_silah*, while they call the end of their line of poetry a *qâfiyah* (rhyme).[28]

However, this comparison is unnecessary as there is no similarity whatsoever between the Qur'ân and Arabic poetry, in any way. Perhaps Al-Jâ_hiz_ was influenced by the allegations of some people that the Qur'ân is nothing but poetry and, therefore, he tried to refute this in relation to the names attributed to both. I believe that he should have saved his efforts as there is no ground for any comparison whatsoever between poetry and the Qur'ân, as has been explained above. Moreover, these names of the Qur'ân and its components were also new terms that were unknown to the pre-Islamic Arabs, a matter which proves the Qur'ân to be beyond human capability and capacity to express ideas.

Aspects of the inimitability of the Qur'ân are extensively varied. Many scholars and rhetoricians in the past and present have written on the inimitability of the Qur'ân, its aspects and manifestations. Al-Suyû_ti_ (849-911 AH), for example, explores thirty-five distinctive aspects or facets of the inimitability of the Qur'ân, all of which are related to only its literary excellence cum supremacy. Whereas some scholars were interested in the way the Qur'ân tells about the *al-ghaib* (the unseen or metaphysics), others were more interested in what can be called the 'rhetoric inimitability' of the Qur'ân. Al-Baqillâni (d. 403 AH), Al-Rummâni (d. 386 AH), Al-Kha_tt_âbi (d. 388 AH), Al-Jurjâni (d. 471 AH), and Al-Râzi

---

[28] Ibid.

(250-311 AH) as well as others wrote extensively on this aspect. There is also a number of modern and contemporary scholars who were interested in writing on the same aspect, such as Al-Rafi`i (1881-1937), Qutb (1906-1966), Drâz (1894-1958), and Bint Al-Shâti' (1913-1998). Interestingly enough, other scholars showed interest in the 'legislative' or 'reformist' inimitability of the Qur'ân, such as Rida (1865-1935) in his *Al-Wahi Al-Muhammadi* (The Revelation to Muhammad).

In addition, a new aspect has recently emerged; it is called the 'scientific' inimitability of the Qur'ân. It refers to recent scientific discoveries that were unknown to man at the time the Qur'ân was revealed, and hence the Qur'ân could be described as being ahead of its time. No one could ever imagine that these discoveries would be foretold by an 'unlettered' person from an illiterate society and in a world void of any tools that make such discoveries possible. Foremost among the most prominent contemporary scholars who write on the scientific inimitability of the Qur'ân are Zaghlul Al-Najjâr (b. 1933) from Egypt and Abdul Majîd Al-Zindâni (b. 1942) from Yemen.

However, the rhetorical inimitability of the Qur'ân is what most serves the purpose of this book and hence deserves attention in a way that does not underestimate any other aspect of this inimitability.

Commenting on the rhetorical inimitability of the Qur'ân, Al-Rafi`i states that when the Arabs encountered the Qur'ân, they found no difference between its terminology and the terminology they used to use. However, the way these terms were put together and even the way the letters comprising these terms were joined were all novel to them. That is why they failed to imitate it and they considered "the style of the Qur'ân is something unlike that which they were familiar with," and hence, it would be impossible for them to produce anything like it. To them, the Qur'ânic style was too perfect to be imitated or copied.[29]

Inimitability of the Qur'ân, as emphasized by Barakah, is an historical fact that can neither be denied nor refuted for lack of proof. The Qur'ân, according to him, truly rendered the Arabs at the time of its revelation helpless to produce anything of its like.[30] This failure to generate anything like the Qur'ân continued until the demise of Prophet Muhammad (peace be upon him). Many centuries have passed since then, and the more time elapses, the stronger and brighter the miracle of the Qur'ân becomes, and the more unlikely the ability of man to imitate or even challenge it becomes. Yet, the Qur'ân is still fresh and still raises the banner of inimitability, challenging all peoples of the world in a very confident and certain manner, as believed by Barakah. The Almighty says,

> {Say to one and all: If all the people and all the
> jinn were to come together to bring about the
> like of the Qur'ân, never would they bring
> about the like of it—even if they were staunch
> backers of one another} (Al-Isrâ' 17: 88).

Indeed, discussing the issue of the inimitability of the Qur'ân is miraculous per se, as whenever any researcher reveals the secrets of any one aspect, other aspects come to the fore with the passage of time. Al-Rafi`i hints at this referring to the great resemblance between the Qur'ân with its inimitable style and the system of this vast universe; scientists have examined this universe from many different angles in various perspectives, yet it is still a new creation to them and attaining a satisfactory understanding of it is, even now, a far-fetched final goal![31]

The Prophet (peace be upon him) challenged the Arabs of his time, who failed to produce anything like the Qur'ân, as

---

[29] Al-Rafi`i, *I`jâz Al-Qur'ân wal-Balaghah al-Nabawiyyah*, 188-190.

[30] Barakah, *Al-I`jâz Al-Qur'âni*, 11.

[31] Al-Rafi`i, *I`jâz Al-Qur'ân wal-Balaghah al-Nabawiyyah*, 140.

has been previously mentioned, though they used to be the mighty masters of eloquence and rhetoric. This, however, cannot be attributed to anything other than the Qur'ân being a miracle.

Earlier scholars, such as Abu Is-hâq Ibrahim Al-Nazzâm (d. 224 AH), Al-Sharif Al-Murtada (d. 436 AH), and Ibn Hazm Al-Andalusi (384-456 AH), claimed that the Qur'ân was inimitable because of *sarfah*, i.e. because Allah, by His Will, turned the people away from producing anything like it. But the fact that no one, since the time of its revelation 1400 years ago, has been able to bring anything even similar to just one *ayah* of this divine book indicates that the Qur'ân is inimitable not only for the Arabs but also for all humankind. Being inimitable up till the present day also indicates that the inimitability of the Qur'ân is due to the uniqueness of the internal composition of the text itself, be it on the level of the word, the sentence, the *ayah*, the *surah*, or the Qur'ân in its entirety, and not due to *sarfah*.

SUGGESTIONS FOR FURTHER READING

For further information on *sarfah*, the reader is kindly referred to Musallam's book, *Mabâhith fi I`jâz Al-Qur'ân*, pp. 58-68.

4 IMPACT OF THE QUR'ÂN ON ARABIC

*"No religious book has had such an impact
on the language in which it was written as
the Qur'ân has had on Arabic literature."*

Jurgi Zaydan (1861-1914)

To many Muslims and lovers of Arabic, the language has acquired a divine touch as the Almighty says in the Qur'ân what means, {Indeed, it is We Ourselves who have sent down the Qur'ân as a revealed Reminder to humanity (of the way of Allah). And, indeed, We Ourselves shall preserve it (it is Our Concern for all time)} (Al-Ḥijr 15: 9). As Allah safeguards His Book, He implicitly safeguards the Arabic language which constitutes the vehicle through which the Qur'ân is transmitted from one generation to another. Consequently, Arabic as a language will last as long as the Qur'ân itself lasts.

In fact, as will be detailed later, Arabic has some unique features that distinguish it from other languages. In this connection, Al-`Aqqâd (1889-1964) stated that the human speech system is a superb musical instrument which no ancient or modern native speakers of any language have used as perfectly as the Arabs. The reason behind this, phonetically speaking, is the fact that native speakers of Arabic use the entire phonetic range in their Arabic alphabet. Therefore, these qualities of the Arabic language are the ones that made Arabic poetry a perfect art that is superior to other arts.[32]

According to Al-`Aqqâd, "these qualities" are not found in any other language, for Arabic eloquence has taken the human speech organs to the highest point ever reached by man in expressing himself using letters and words.[33]

Another scholar admits that no one can find any other language that appeared to scholars so complete and without gradation, retaining a structure so pure and flawless, except Arabic.[34]

Here, a brief account follows on some of the significant effects the Qur'ân has had on the Arabic language:

A. Preserving Arabic from Extinction

No doubt, the Qur'ân is crucially essential to the life of all Muslims. That is why many Muslims dedicate themselves to serving the Qur'ân. In so doing, they defend the Arabic language and consider any attack against it as targeting the Qur'ân itself, and *vice versa*. Muslims defend the Qur'ân because it is the first main source of their faith, followed by the *Sunnah* of Prophet Muḥammad (peace be upon him). In a similar vein, they defend Arabic for it constitutes the basic means required for understanding the message of the Qur'ân. Hence, the preservation of Arabic up till now is a result of defending as well as preserving the Qur'ân itself.

Al-Baquri (1907-1985) argued that had the Qur'ân been

---

[32] Al-`Aqqad, *Al-Lughah Al-Sha`irah,* 70.
[33] Ibid.
[34] Al-Jindi, *Al-Fuṣ-ḥa: Lughat Al-Qur'ân,* 27.

revealed in the same form as the previous divine books, i.e. in the form of pieces of wisdom, ordinances, promises and threats, without this inimitable style, no one would have been interested in caring for its words, style, and rhetoric. Consequently, Arabic, the language in which the Qur'ân was revealed, would have become obsolete and deserted even by its own native speakers as time passed.[35]

To validate his argument, Al-Baquri argued that even though Hebrew was the original language of a divine book, i.e. the Torah, it has become obsolete. Had the Children of Israel been challenged by the Torah, just as the Arabs were challenged by the Qur'ân, they would have endeavored to preserve their language and keep it intact—consequently preserving the miracle of their Prophet. We would then have seen the language of Musa (Moses) (peace be upon him) alive today, but it is not as no one can claim that present-day Hebrew is the same language that was spoken by Prophet Musa (peace be upon him) and his people several centuries ago.[36]

To conclude, in its capacity as a human language, Arabic is vulnerable to change, alteration and extinction. The Qur'ân, in its capacity as the lasting miracle of Islam, is the factor that has and will preserve Arabic and save it from dying out. This is because it overtly challenged the Arabs to produce just one *ayah* like it, but they admitted their utter failure. Hence, Muslims directed their efforts to the words of the Qur'ân by memorizing and studying the different aspects of its inimitability. Were the Qur'ân revealed in the same form as the previous divine books, the fate of its language would not have been any different from theirs!

---

[35] Al-Baquri, *Athar Al-Qur'ân Al-Karim fi Al-Lughah Al-`Arabiyyah,* 33.

[36] Ibid., 33-34.

B. Strengthening the Arabic Language

The strength and richness the Qur'ân gave to the Arabic language could have never been attained by any other means. Since Arabic is the medium of Qur'ânic revelation, it has become a major attraction to many non-Arabs who found it prestigious to learn. Arabic strength, widespread use, and vitality were noted by the famous French Orientalist, Ernest Renan (1823-1894), who carried out extensive research on Semitic languages. He said about the development of Arabic that it is the most astonishing event of human history. Unknown during the pre-Islamic period, it suddenly emerged as a complete language. After this, it did not undergo any noticeable changes, so it is impossible to define an early or a late stage for it; it is just the same today as it was when it first appeared.[37]

In acknowledging this "astonishing event of human history", Renan is in fact acknowledging the miraculous nature of the Qur'ân. It was the Qur'ân's phenomenal literary style which preserved the Arabic language from the alteration that affected nearly all other languages.

In addition and as further evidence on the strength of the Arabic language, the Christian, Jurgi Zaydan (1861-1914), stated in his book on Arabic literature, "No religious book has had such an impact on the language in which it was written as the Qur'ân has had on Arabic literature."[38]

Finally, yet importantly, those quotes by non-Muslim scholars have been stated here to highlight the fact that the matter of recognizing the strength of the Arabic language is not restricted to Muslims alone, and to also avoid any sense of potential bias.

---

[37] Al-Jindi, *Al-Fuṣ-ḥa: Lughat Al-Qur'ân,* 27.
[38] Khan, www.alrisala.org.

C. Standardization of Arabic Tribal Dialects

Classical Arabic had many different dialects during the pre- and earlier Islamic periods. Some of these dialects were more eloquent and superior to others; but others were disliked. However, all Arab tribes took justifiable pride in their own dialects; hence, the Qur'ân was revealed in seven modes of recitation to make its recitation and understanding easy for all the Arabs.

Again, Arabic dialects were not equal in terms of eloquence and rhetoric supremacy. Caliph `Uthmân ibn `Affân (47 BH-35 AH) was aware of this when he endeavored to collect the Qur'ân as he told the committee appointed for the task, "In case of dispute among yourselves, you should write it down in conformity with the dialect of Quraish because it [the Qur'ân] was revealed in their dialect." This is because the dialect of Quraish was the easiest, the clearest, and the most eloquent among all Arabic dialects. It also reflected all the dialects of different tribes because Makkah was the center where all Arabs used to gather to perform Hajj (Pilgrimage), exchange trade, and participate in the regularly held literary competitions of that time.

Consequently, the Qur'ân unified the different tribes and made all Arabs a single *ummah* (community, nation) which uses the same language. Al-Rafi`i explained the reason behind this by saying that the Qur'ân made all those Arabs use one single variety of the language, as it encompasses all the subtle aspects that could ever be found in the language; a matter which convinced all Arabs from different tribes to use it and not replace it at any time with any other language variety.[39]

Hence, according to Al-Rafi`i, the Arabs were encouraged to attend to the style of the Qur'ân as well as its vocabulary due to the intrinsic superiority they felt therein that discouraged them from using anything which was of a lower standard.

---

[39] Al-Rafi`i, *I`jâz Al-Qur'ân wal-Balaghah al-Nabawiyyah*, 78.

D. Turning Arabic into a Universal Language

According to Al-Baquri, no one can deny that "language is an honest reflection of its users' life."[40] Before the revelation of the Qur'ân, the Arabs were unknown to other nations. Their language did not attract others as it was neither a language of knowledge nor civilization. Consequently, Arabic was forced to stay in its cradle, reaching out to no other region beyond its geographical borders.

The Arabs remained as such until the Qur'ân brought the noblest and loftiest principles and values ever known to man. The Qur'ân also called upon the Arabs to call others to the true faith. It is understood that upon accepting Islam as one's faith, a person should exert himself to learn Arabic to be able to observe the prescribed religious rituals and acts of worship. As a result, numerous people started to learn Arabic, the language of the Qur'ân—a matter without which Arabic would not have witnessed this wide-spread and extended fame.

Ascertaining this, Al-Baquri says that Arabic would not have had any reason to leave the Arabian Peninsula to compete with and even overcome languages of the civilized nations at that time. However, it is the Qur'ân that delivered it from the arms of the desert and paved its way to a spacious kingdom from which it acquired new words and novel meanings, purposes and styles.

E. Written Description of the Rules of Arabic

Unlike the present day, Arabs of pre-Islamic era used to acquire their language naturally, as they had no recorded prescriptive grammatical rules. There was no need at that time of such rules or systematic education as it sufficed them to acquire the language by intuition. Many earlier scholars, such as Al-Shâfi`i (150-204 AH), declared that their competence

---

[40] Al-Baquri, *Athar Al-Qur'ân Al-Karim fi Al-Lughah Al-`Arabiyyah*, 42-49.

and performance of Arabic improved only when they were sent to learn intact and pure Classical Arabic from the Bedouins.

Later on, Arabs came in direct contact with non-Arab Muslims who started to distort Arabic through faulty unauthentic usage. That was one of the reasons Caliph `Uthmân ordered the Qur'ân to be collected in one manuscript in conformity to the established modes of recitation. Fear and anxiety about reciting the Qur'ân incorrectly by new non-Arab Muslims stirred Abu Al-Aswad Al-Du'ali (16 BH-69 AH) to write the first manuscript of Arabic grammar.

Furthermore, unlike many other languages, Arabic orthography was kept intact. In this regard, `Itir remarked that the way of representing writing in the Qur'ân became the standard. Orthographical rules of Arabic developed to better reflect precision and accurate pronunciation.[41] Thus, thanks to the Qur'ân, the method of writing Arabic was maintained and no alteration whatsoever from the written characters of the ancestors has ever been witnessed.

Moreover, Arabic was a well-established language that used to be acquired naturally by pre-Islamic Arabs, as has been mentioned earlier. However, following the advent of Islam, the Arabs went outside the borders of the Arabian Peninsula and mixed with non-Arabs. Consequently, their ability to use this language of theirs began to weaken; hence, the following generations needed to learn Arabic. They, at the same time, needed to teach the non-Arab Muslims the language by which they could understand the Qur'ân. Consequently, the need for recording the grammatical rules emerged to circumvent the learning difficulties encountered by both the non-Arab Muslims and the Arabs of the following generations. A more detailed discussion of this topic can be found under the Chapter titled: *The Development of Arabic Linguistics.*

---

[41] `Itir, *Al-Qur'ân al-Karim wal Dirasat al-Adabiyyah*, 361.

F. Refining Arabic Terminology

The language of a nation is an honest reflection of the nature as well as public taste of its users. If geographical location has an impact on the inborn character of its inhabitants, the speakers of a language also affect their language. Al-Rafi`i stated that language and the character of its native speakers are inseparable. They are perfect matches in terms of their strengths and weaknesses.[42] This is because language is a verbal representation of its users' ideas, while the users have the ability to represent speech as an image. Language can be seen as words that represent the users' ideas, and the users can be seen as being those who give images and meanings to speech. Hence, it is clear that both are intrinsically connected.

This is proved to be valid by reading the history of the Muslim Ummah (nation) side-by side with that of the Arabic Language; such an analysis reveals the co-relation between times of strength and weakness.

In fact, the Arabs were based in the desert and thus their language was characterized by coarseness, except for the tribe of Quraish whose language was milder as they were urbanites. This was indicated in their literary production. Anyone who reads pre-Islamic poetry will find strange and coarse words, except in the literature of the Quraishites.

Not only did the Qur'ân move the Arabs from the coarseness and roughness of the desert to the mildness and softness of urbanism, but it also selected its own words from among the mildest and most eloquent of all. This made Ibn Khalawaih (d. 370 AH) say that there is a consensus among all Muslim scholars that if something is mentioned in the Qur'ân, it must be more correct and appropriate than the way it is mentioned elsewhere. Al-Rafi`i also stated that the Qur'ân refined the Arabic language and removed its coarseness.[43]

---

[42] Al-Rafi`i , *I`jâz Al-Qur'ân wal-Balaghah al-Nabawiyyah*, 75.
[43] Ibid.

SUGGESTIONS FOR FURTHER READING

For further readings on the impact of the Qur'ân on Arabic, one is referred to `Abd Al-Sabur Shahin (1986), *Al-`Arabiyyah Lughat Al-`Ulûm wal Taqniyyah*, (Arabic: The Language of Science and Technology), Cairo, Dar Al-I`tisâm, pp. 59-63.

5 FEATURES OF ARABIC GRAMMAR

*"Arabic is thus a language of rare breadth
and extension in the world, a language like
perhaps no other in the degree to which it
embodies the culture and politics of its
speakers."*

Jonathan Owens (2013)

Arabic has a number of unique features that make it distinct from all other languages, especially those of Indo-European origin. These features may constitute some sort of complexity to those concerned with constructing a computational system to research Arabic. This chapter, however, may serve as an introduction to the problems encountered when attempting to search the Arabic texts using computers. Some of these unique features are related to grammar and script and can be summarized as follows:

Arabic Grammar

This section is mostly adapted from (Thompson 2016) who said that one of the basic features of Arabic grammar is that Arabic nouns are marked for definiteness/indefiniteness.[44] Definiteness is marked by the article '*al*' (the), while indefiniteness is usually indicated by the suffix '*n*' which follows the case marker. This feature is present in all dialects of Arabic, e.g.,

Nominative + definite	*Al-kitab-u*	'the book'
Nominative (indefinite)	*Kitab-un*	'a book'

Arabic has three number categories: singular, dual, and plural. The dual number is normally used to refer to two objects, and both the dual and the plural are usually formed by adding a suffix to the end of a word. In some instances, the plural is expressed by changing the vowel structure of a word, e.g., *kitâb*, 'book', *kutub*, 'books'. This is called *jam`taksîr* (broken plural).

Arabic has two genders: masculine and feminine. Adjectives, pronouns, and verbs agree with nouns in case, gender and number.

In addition, the verb system of Arabic is difficult to describe from the perspective of Indo-European languages. Some of its most salient features are listed below:

-Person, mood, and aspect are marked by prefixes and suffixes.

-There is one basic stem plus nine derived stems, each with a range of meanings, such as reflexivity and

---

[44] Thompson, *Arabic,* www.aboutworldlanguages.com/arabic-modern-standard.

causativity. Each form has its own set of active and passive participles and verbal nouns.

As far as tense is concerned, Arabic has a past (or perfect) suffixed conjugation and a non-past (or imperfect) prefixed conjugation. The perfect can refer to present or future. The imperfect can refer to present, past, or future.

The normal word order in Classical Arabic is *Verb-Subject-Object*, while the usual word order in colloquial varieties is *Subject-Verb-Object*. Amazingly enough, MSA now also relies on a *Subject-Verb-Object* word order.

Regarding Arabic vocabulary, it is formed by applying vowels and affixes to three-consonant roots, for example, the root *K-T-B* produces '*kitâb*' (book) and '*kâtib*' (writer). According to Thalouth et al. (1986), around 64% of roots are composed of three consonants.[45] The other roots consist of two, four and five consonants. The system that studies how words are constructed from roots and describes the patterns they follow is called *sarf* (Arabic Morphology).

Arabic Script

Unlike Western languages, Arabic is written from right to left. The Arabic alphabet is an accurate representation of the sound system of the language, which contains 28 symbols. In addition to these 28 symbols, there are other letters or symbols in loanwords that contain sounds that do not naturally occur in Arabic, e.g., /p/ and /g/. The basic features of the Arabic script can be summarized as follows:

- It is consonant-based.

- Words are written in horizontal lines from right to left.

- Most letters change their shape depending on their position in a word. The shape of some letters allows

---

[45] Khoja et al., *A tagset for the morphological tagging of Arabic*, 59-60.

them to be joined to the following letter in the word, while the shape of others does not. Letters that can be joined are always joined in both handwritten and printed Arabic. All but six letters can be attached to the following letter. These six letters are: ١ (a), د (d), ذ (dh), ر (r), ز (z), and و (w).

- Unlike Western languages, Arabic has no capital letters.

- Arabic letters are simplified in handwritten form.

- As for vowel diacritics which represent short vowels, they are used in a small number of texts. Foremost among these texts are the Qur'ân, religious texts, classical poetry, children's books and textbooks for learners of Arabic. However, this feature is highly problematic, as stated by Al-Daimi et al. (1994), "For technical reasons the discretization is impossible when using the computer. This results in compound cases of morphological-lexical and morphological-syntactical ambiguities."[46] However, it is believed that this problem has been solved in the last decade by many software companies who are interested in researching Arabic using computers.

- Unlike English, which is more analytic, Arabic is a synthetic (i.e. inflectional) language. Three cases are always associated with Arabic: nominative, accusative and genitive. The case system in Arabic is problematic as all three cases are represented by short vowels but the Arabic script on computers only allows the writer to show consonants and long vowels. Diacritics, which are traditionally used for case endings, are computationally problematic, as has been stated earlier.

- Pronouns in Arabic are allowed to combine with words to form one single new word. Such personal pronouns can be suffixed to nouns, verbs or particles. One Arabic

---

[46] AlDaimi & Abdel-Amir, *The syntactic analysis of Arabic by machine*, 29.

word can represent a complete meaningful sentence. Consider the following word:

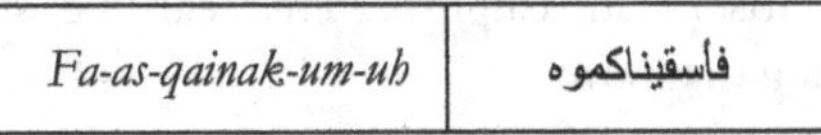

Fa-as-qainak-um-uh	فأسقيناكموه

{…and thus We give it to you to drink} (Al-Hijr 15: 22).

This feature gives rise to another problematic issue when attempting to computationally research Arabic; when searching for a word in an electronic text, i.e. a corpus, the researcher has to search for every possible form of this word. This is because, if his search is restricted to the stem of a given word, an unnecessarily huge number of results will emerge; adding to the complexities usually encountered when analyzing Arabic.

- The Arabic language is an inflectional language whereas English is an analytic language. The derivation in Arabic is based on morphological patterns and the verb plays a greater inflectional role than verbs in English. Furthermore, Arabic words are derived from roots resulting in the formation of word families having lexically and semantically connected elements. This is not the case with English, which uses the stem as a basis for word generation.[47]

- Every lexical set in Arabic has some letters and sounds in common. All words derived from one Arabic root share a fundamental meaning. Nevertheless, English words do not enjoy this privilege. The root /B N W/ in Arabic refers to the English word (son), while /B N T/ in Arabic refers to the English word (daughter). This characteristic of the Arabic language helps detect any unusual word that attempts to penetrate into its lexicon at any point of time.

- Arabic offers the possibility of combining particles and affixed pronouns to words, whereas this possibility is totally absent in English. This can be shown in the following diagram:

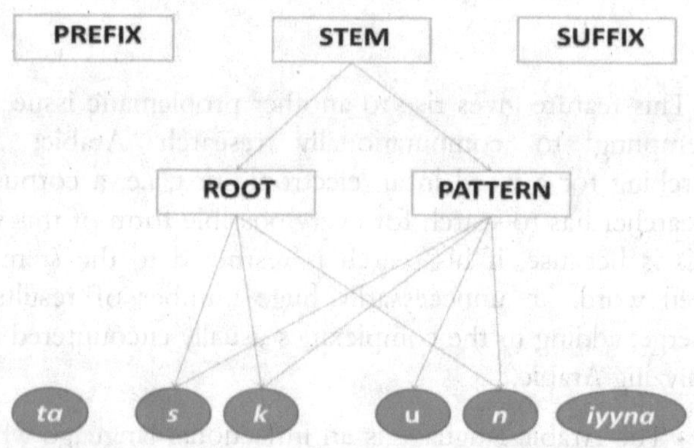

Diagram 1: Morphological structure for an Arabic word
'*taskuniyyna*' (you live in).

- English imposes a large number of constraints on word order. However, Arabic is distinguished for its high syntactical flexibility, which allows a great deal of freedom in the ordering of words in sentences.

SUGGESTIONS FOR FURTHER READING

For further information on the characteristics of Arabic and its potentials, one is better referred to Ghunaim (1990): *Al-Lughah Al-`Arabiyyah wal Sahwah Al-`Ilmiyyah Al-Hadithah*, (The Arabic Language and Modern Scientific Awakening), Ibn Sina Bookstore, pp. 39-54.

6 THE DEVELOPMENT OF ARABIC LINGUISTICS

"The first comprehensive description of the ʿarabiyya "Arabic", Sibawayhi's al-Kitab, is based first of all upon a corpus of poetic texts, in addition to the Qurʾan and Bedouin informants whom he considered to be reliable speakers of the ʿarabiyya."

Encyclopedia of Arabic Language and Linguistics (2011)

The Arabic language originated in the Arabian Peninsula in pre-Islamic times and spread rapidly to different parts of the world due to the rapid spread of Islam.

Before Islam, the Arabs were Bedouins who used to roam throughout the Arabian Peninsula. They spoke the same language but there were various dialects; a matter which resulted in some slight alterations in the language from one tribe to another. To them, language was "a habit of their tongues which they transmit from one another."[48]

However, many Arabs left their homeland after the spread of Islam and were thus in contact with non-Arabs, as has been stated earlier. Later on, Arabic started to undergo some change or decay as incorrect usages appeared on the tongues of the non-Arab reverts with whom the Arabs mixed. Consequently, Muslim scholars began to fear that Arabic might become completely corrupted. Their fear was that this might eventually render the Qur'ân and the Prophet's Tradition incomprehensible by those who had become familiar with the corrupted Arabic. To avoid this, they invented what was later called `Ilm Al-Nahw (The Science of Grammar).

Arabic linguistics emerged in the seventh century AC. According to many reports, the Arabs were shocked by the mistakes made by reverts and thus attempted to codify the norms of correct linguistic usage to preserve their pure language from decay. Two famous stories are related in this regard. One story involves the governor of Iraq, Ziyad ibn Abîhi (1-53 AH), and the second involves the fourth Caliph, `Ali ibn Abî Tâlib (23 BH-40 AH), both of whom requested the assistance of a well-known scholar, Abul Aswad Al-Du'ali, for this task.

To cite one of the two stories, Al-Du'ali himself can be quoted as saying:

> "I came to the Commander of the Believers `Ali ibn Abî Tâlib and saw in his hand a manuscript. I said to him, 'What is this, Commander of the Believers?' He said, 'I was reflecting on the language of the Arabs and noted that it had been corrupted by our mixing with these red persons—i.e. foreigners—and I wanted to make something for them on which they could fall back and on which they could rely.' Then

---

[48] Versteegh, *Greek translations of the Quran in Christian polemics*, 143.

> he handed me the manuscript that said that language is made up of nouns, verbs and particles. The noun is what informs us about a named object; the verb describes the movement of the named object; and the particle is neither a noun nor a verb but its meaning is understood from its relationship to the words that precede or follow it. He said to me, 'Follow this directive and add thereto whatever you find!'"[49]

Regardless of the authenticity of these reports about Al-Du'ali, it is certain that the Arabic grammar was written to help prevent the decay that started to affect some aspects of Arabic at the hands of non-Arabs who started to take it as their second language.

Several attempts have been made to link the origin of Arabic grammar to foreign linguistic traditions such as Greek or Indian; however, there is nothing that bolsters these claims. On the contrary, Eliwa argued that "[T]he science [Arabic linguistics] was founded before the beginning of the great movement of translation from other languages into Arabic during the Umayyad and Abbasid eras."[50] It goes without saying that Caliph `Alî ibn Abî Ṭâlib had no opportunity to come in contact with the traditions of the Greeks or Indians; the correct view is that he is the one who was the true founder of Arabic linguistics.

The golden age of Arabic linguistics, as believed by many linguists, was between the 8th and 11th centuries. It is believed that "[I]n the 12th and 13th centuries, Arabic was looked upon with admiration by the West in the same manner the Arab of today looks at the more developed Western languages."[51]

Owens argued that the study of Arabic linguistics and its

---

[49] Ibn Al-Anbari as quoted in Versteegh, *Greek translations of the Quran in Christian polemics*, 4.

[50] Eliwa, *Synonymy and lexical collocation in classical Arabic*, 17.

[51] Chejne, 170, as quoted in Eliwa, *Synonymy and lexical collocation in classical Arabic*, 17.

methodology was at its best and most sophisticated level at the time of Al-Jurjâni.[52] He believed that all later contributions were mainly interested in remodeling or making slight changes to what had been carried out in the early centuries of Islam.

Stressing the same point of remodeling and elucidating the earlier contributions, Versteegh claimed, "[T]he entire linguistic tradition in Arabic is nothing but a huge commentary on the *Kitâb Sibawâyh* (the Book of Sibawâyh)."[53] He also stated that one biographer called it *Qur'ân al-Naḥw* (The Qur'ân of Grammar), like the phrase '*The Bible of such and such*' in English, meaning, 'a book considered to be authoritative in its field'. In a similar vein, Sibawâyh himself was believed by Ghali to be the *Imam al-Nuḥâh* (Leader of the Grammarians).[54]

This is because of the uniqueness of his book in two respects: (a) it was the first coherent description of the rules of the Arabic language; and (b) it was one of the first publications about Arabic heritage in any discipline at a time when publications were astonishingly scarce.

I believe that after Sibawâyh, the later grammarians engaged themselves in expounding his theory in a more explicit and systematic manner. This incites me to say that little contribution has been made in the past millennium in the field of Arabic linguistics. The trend in the early 20th Century depended totally on the linguistic legacy of earlier Arab grammarians and involved verifying and editing the earlier grammarians' manuscripts, and explaining and expounding their works using modern linguistic terminology.

However, the Arabic language seems to have experienced a change in this pattern in the last four decades. Many

---

[52] Owens, as quoted in Eliwa, *Synonymy and lexical collocation in classical Arabic*, 17.

[53] Versteegh, *Greek translations of the Quran in Christian polemics*, 39.

[54] Ghali, *A'imat Al-Nuḥah*.

researchers are now more interested in examining Arabic by adopting and applying modern linguistic theories and research methods. Much of the work in this field has been carried out in thesis or dissertation form, both in the universities of the Arab world and abroad, some of which have been published.

As linguistics in the United States and Europe flourished and took on another dimension after the advent of the computer, the same surge affected Arabic as many researchers tried to apply these modern techniques—especially those of the corpus linguistics—to the Arabic language.

After this brief overview of the Arabic language and the impact the Qur'ân had on it, it is now time to look into the second part of this book, which is concerned with the translation of the meanings of the Qur'ân into English. What the translation of the Qur'ân means; the types of translation in relation to the Qur'ân; the problems encountered by different translators and more will be detailed further in PART TWO.

PART TWO

TRANSLATION
OF THE QUR'ÂNIC TEXT

7 TRANSLATION AND THE QUR'ÂN

"The Koran undeniably abounds in fine writing. It has its own extremely individual qualities; the language is highly idiomatic, yet for the most part delusively simple; and the rhythms and rhymes are inseparable features of its impressive eloquence which are indeed inimitable."

A. J. Arberry (1905–1969)

Translation is neither easy, nor is it one of the 'sciences' to be learnt or mastered with little or no effort. Catford defined translation as, "the replacement of textual material in one language (SL) by equivalent textual material in another language (TL)".[55] This definition may imply that translation is an easy task. However, this is not the case as translation requires patience,

---

[55] Catford, *A linguistic theory of translation*, 20.

persistence, and the will to learn and accumulate experiences. To be rightly called a 'translator', one should first master the SL as well as the TL to a highly remarkable degree.

Mastering a language does not only imply knowing its lexical entries and rules of grammar, but it also implies awareness of the culture represented by that language and even its history. Abu Laylah stated, "All languages have their own structures and systems of meaning dependent on culturally based or individually recognized forces. Language is, to a degree, not directly and purely translatable."[56] This prerequisite of the translator–to know all about the language he is translating into or from–makes his responsibility even greater.

This is the case for all human languages as they all share this same difficulty. However, if Arabic is part of the process, i.e. the translation task, an additional load is shouldered by the translator. This is because Arabic, as has been elaborated on earlier, has well-known unique features that render translation from Arabic into any other language and *vice versa* more than difficult.

Translating the Untranslatable

As for the Qur'ân, Muslims believe that it can only be read in the language in which it was revealed, namely Arabic. Anything else is just a translation of its meaning, and not the divine words of Allah. The significance of translating the meaning of the Qur'ân emanates from the importance of the Qur'ân itself, as it ranks first among the two main sources of the Muslim faith. Hence, it is no wonder that one sees a huge number of essays, books, and critical studies addressing the various translations that have been contributed by a large number of translators.

The Qur'ânic text to some scholars, such as Pickthall, is

---

[56] Abu Laylah, *The Qur'ân and the Gospels: A comparative study*, 57.

untranslatable; to put it in his own words, "The *Koran* cannot be translated." That is his and the "old-fashioned Sheikhs" belief, as he said. He further explained that his book was rendered almost literarily, and that he exerted himself to choose the most fitting language. However, "The result is not the Glorious *Koran*, that inimitable symphony, the very sounds of which move men to tears and ecstasy."[57]

In his preface to the second edition of his translation of the meaning of the Qur'ân, Ghali stated, "The Qur'ân is untranslatable." He attributed the untranslatability of the Qur'ân to the fact that "[N]o human medium can reproduce the dignity and divine glory of the Arabic revelation." However, he admitted that each translation has its "distinctive value."[58]

Arberry argued that "The *Koran* undeniably abounds in fine writing. It has its own extremely individual qualities; the language is highly idiomatic, yet for the most part delusively simple; and the rhythms and rhymes are inseparable features of its impressive eloquence which are indeed inimitable."[59]

He further argued that the Qur'ân "is neither prose nor poetry, but a unique fusion of both."[60] It is his belief that the rhetoric and rhythm of the Qur'ân are so distinctive, powerful, and emotive that any translation is just a poor copy of the glorious original.

Tibawi strictly opposed any attempt to translate the Qur'ân into any other language. He argued that "Arabic is abundant in metaphors, and no language could rival it in this sense." He stated that it "is unanimous; [all scholars agree] that it is virtually impossible to translate Arabic into any language, still less to translate the Arabic of the Qur'ân."[61] In

---

[57] Pickthall, *The meaning of the glorious Qur'ân.*

[58] Ghali, *Towards understanding the ever-glorious Qur'ân*, i.

[59] Arberry, *The holy Koran: An introduction with selections*, 28.

[60] Arberry, *The Koran interpreted: A translation*, x.

[61] Tibawi, *Is the translation of the Qur'ân possible? Early Muslim opinions*, 17-28.

the same vein, in his book *Al-Hayawân*, Al-Jâhiz maintained that it is impossible to translate Arabic poetry into any language, and that it is better not to attempt to translate any material dealing with religion and the Qur'ân.[62]

Abdul-Raof used 'shifting' or 'reference switching' to illustrate the fact that the Qur'ânic discourse is characterized by various syntactic, semantic, rhetorical, and cultural features that are distinct from other types of Arabic discourse. To him, these features are untranslatable, and hence, he stresses the untranslatability of the Qur'ân.[63]

Similarly, Bultemeier argued that the translation of the Qur'ân into any language is "impossible" for a number of reasons. Firstly, the translation must maintain the same effect on the reader of the TL as the original text of the Qur'ân, but the Qur'ânic *ayahs* lose the same symphonic effect if translated into any other language. Secondly, to him, the Qur'ân contains Syriac and Aramaic vocabulary, a matter which is unusual to Arabic. This increases the complexity of the translation process since the meaning of certain phrases is not clear, and different interpretations are possible.[64]

Arbuthnot stated, "From the literary point of view, the *Koran* is regarded as a specimen of the purest Arabic, written in half poetry and half prose." According to him, grammarians have adapted their rules to agree with certain phrases and expressions used therein, and though many have attempted to produce something equal to it, "As far elegant writing is concerned, none have, as yet, succeeded."[65]

It is clear that the inimitable rhetoric of the Qur'ân has been unanimously declared impossible to translate. Notwithstanding, the possibility of transferring its meaning into other languages is still maintained. Thereupon, the

---

[62] Al-Jâhiz, *Al-Hayawan*, 74-79.

[63] Abdul-Raof, *Quran translation: Discourse, texture and exegesis*.

[64] Al-Jabari, *Reasons for the possible incomprehensibility of some verses of three translations of the meaning of the holy Quran into English*, 20.

[65] Arbuthnot, *The construction of the Bible and the Koran*, 245.

objective of the translation process should only be for missionary (*da`wah*) purposes.

Qur'ân translation history is quite long and the list of translations contributed so far is endless, as new translations constantly appear. In his attempt to numerate these translations, Al-Lawindi concluded, "It is said that the translations of the Qur'ân into the different world languages amount to more than 700 translations up till now".[66] However, surveying and/or assessing these translations is not the aim of this present book.

Types of Translation with reference to the Qur'ân

Three types of translation can be distinguished when discussing the case of the Qur'ân: literal, meaning-based (i.e., non-literal), and interpretive translations.

Literal Translation

This is word-for-word translation. In Al-Qattân's words, "It is to transfer [a set of] lexical items from one language to their matches in another language, so that both the style [of the text] and the order [of the lexical items] become identical."[67] However, this proves to be almost impossible between any two languages. As far as the Islamic *sharî`ah* is concerned, this type of translation is neither possible nor legal, except for the *ayahs* which can be literally translated.[68]

Literal translation renders only the denotative meaning of the lexical item as it is listed in the dictionary. Certainly, the connotative meaning of an Arabic word differs from that of an English word, even if their denotative meanings are almost the same. Consequently, the rendered meaning fails to

---

[66] Al-Lawindi, *Ishkaliyat Tarjamat Ma`ani Al-Qur'ân Al-Karim*, 19.
[67] Al-Qattan, *Mabahith fi `Ulûm Al-Qur'ân*, 324.
[68] Zaqzuq, *Al-Mawsu`ah al-Qur'âniyyah al-Mutakhasisah*, 863-866.

transfer not only the genuine meaning, but also the general context of the ST. Attesting to this, Dickins et al. stated, "Meanings are not found exclusively in the words listed individually in the dictionary."[69]

Hence, literal translation neglects the subtle meanings with which the Qur'ânic text is replete. Even with a cursory investigation, it becomes clear that this type of translation is unable to attend to the inimitable style and structure of the Qur'ân, which cannot be maintained even in Arabic with other non-Qur'ânic terms.

In other words, the difficulties ensuing from the literal translation of the Qur'ân into other languages stem from the Qur'ân's inimitable wording—a matter which renders its translation impossible unless it is restricted to its basic meaning or the personal interpretation of the translator. In addition, the Qur'ân's magnificent rhyme, eloquence, and style that deeply impress man's soul are lost in the literal translation.

Meaning-Based Translation

This refers to rendering "the meaning of a text in another language by neither abiding by the order of the lexical items in the original text, nor by its structure," as explained by Al-Qattân.[70]

All eloquent Arabic texts, topped by the Qur'ân, have basic and secondary meanings. The basic meaning stands for the conclusive type of meanings or messages which anyone can understand once he understands the meaning of the word in use. There is a high possibility that such meanings can be conveyed into any other language. However, and particularly with the Qur'ân, there are also secondary or implicit meanings

---

[69] Dickins et al., *Thinking Arabic translation, a course in translation method: Arabic to English*, 97.

[70] Al-Qattan, *Mabahith fi `Ulûm Al-Qur'ân*, 324.

which are almost impossible to translate into another language, especially if one takes into consideration the eloquence of the text. This type of meaning is what testifies to the inimitability of the Qur'ân. Arguing for this, Al-Zamakhshari stated, "Indeed, there are in the Arabic language in general and in the Qur'ân in particular subtle implicit meanings that cannot be expressed by any other language."[71]

Al-Shatibi dichotomized the meanings portrayed in all languages, including Arabic. The first include "the general terms and expressions which denote broad meanings and constitute the basic or abstract meaning of these terms and expressions," while the second include "the specific terms denoting secondary, implicit meanings." According to him, it is the first type that is common among all languages and which enables humans to communicate. Consequently, translation at this level from Arabic into other languages is "possible."[72]

However, this overgeneralization concerning the validity of translation based on only the basic meaning is opposed by Al-Qattân, who stated that some scholars see translation as permissible only in case of necessity, such as the need to convey the message of *tawhîd* (Islamic monotheism) and/or teach the `*ibadât* (acts of worship), and nothing more. He concluded, "As for those who crave to obtain more knowledge, they should be encouraged to learn Arabic."[73]

Remarkably, most translations of the Qur'ân into the different world languages can safely be attributed to this type, i.e., meaning-based translation. There are a few exceptions to this as some contributors felt the deficiencies of this type. To make up for these deficiencies, they added illustrative remarks and basic comments which they considered necessary, in the footnotes. Yusuf Ali's translation suffices as an example of this.

---

[71] Al-Zamakhshari, *Al-Kashshaf,* 476.

[72] Al-Shatibi, *Al-Muwafaqat fi Usûl al-Sharî`ah,* 56-57.

[73] Al-Qattan, *Mabahith fi `Ulûm Al-Qur'ân,* 326.

However, almost all translations contain interpretations of some expressions and terms that fail to transfer their denotative as well as connotative meanings.

Interpretive Translation

This is when a translator finds it impossible to transfer the entire meaning of the Qur'ânic terms and expressions. Hence, he/she develops a personal understanding of the text at hand, and then sets out to render this understanding into the TL.[74]

In this sense, interpretive translation is different from the meaning-based one, though they might be confused with each other. The latter gives the false impression that the translator has grasped all the meanings of the Qur'ân and was successful in transferring them all into the TL. It is as if one says, "This is exactly what the *ayah* means!" Whereas the translator, in the interpretive type, attempts to reproduce the text as per his personal understanding of it; as if he says, "This is what I think the *ayah* means!"

Stressing the validity of this method which is deemed by Al-Lawindi as a "must" in light of the difficulty of both the literal and meaning-based translations, he argued that if Muslims neglect the issue of translating the Qur'ân, they would be without any "reference or support" in many regions of the world. They would end up finding an Arabic Qur'ân in their hands which they truly "respect," but of which they "basically comprehend nothing!" To him, the natural consequence of this is that the meaning of the Qur'ân will remain "incomprehensible to many nations," a matter which is both unfair and contradictory to the universality of Islam.[75]

To Al-Shabab, translation is merely "an interpretative (hermeneutic) behavior." This interpretive nature of translation is destined to give rise to "differences" in

---

⁷⁴ Ibid., 327-328.
⁷⁵ Al-Lawindi, *Ishkaliyat Tarjamat Ma`ani Al-Qur'ân Al-Karim*, 40.

translation.[76]

O'Donnell also stated, "Every translation is an interpretation, and therefore, even when making a quick initial translation, the exegete is forced to make interpretative decisions."[77] This conforms to Levy, who advocated translation "as a decision process."[78] It is "a dynamic process of comprehension and re-expression of ideas," as deemed by Salama-Carr.[79]

Significance of an Interpretive Translation

Translating the terms and expressions comprising the Qur'ân is, by definition, challenging. It becomes nearly impossible if one wishes to simultaneously provide equivalents for all the meanings denoted by and associated with the term in its textual context. In other words, it would be impossible for any translator, regardless of his/her competence and skill, to render both explicit and implicit meanings of the Qur'ânic terms and expressions. Hence, the need arises for a methodical procedure that may enable the translator(s) to fully understand the meaning of these terms without causing any loss in translation. Under the heading, *Golden rules for translating the Qur'ân*, I propose an eight-point scheme for the translation of the Qur'ân in a way that may reduce the translator's personal influence or presumptions in relation to what is denoted and/or connoted by the different elements of the sacred text.

The more the translators understand the text, the more they become aware of their own incompetence and the insufficiency of any other language to express the same sort of inimitability involved. Ayyoûb noted,

---

[76] Al-Shabab, *Translating with difference: Theory and practice.*

[77] O'Donnell, *Translation and the exegetical process,* 165.

[78] Levy, *Translation as a decision process,* vol. 2.

[79] Salama-Carr, *Interpretive Approach,* in Baker et al., (ed.) Routledge Encyclopaedia of Translation Studies, 146.

> "Because the Qur'ân stresses its Arabic nature, Muslim scholars believe that any translation cannot be more than an approximate interpretation intended only as a tool for the study and understanding of the original Arabic."[80]

Moreover, Bewley & Bewley (2005) argued that Allah "chose pure, Classical Arabic as the linguistic vehicle" for His Book because of its "unique capacity to retain and convey a great depth of meaning in a multi-faceted way" which goes beyond "the scope of any other language."[81]

In other words, the Arabic terms and/or concepts used in the Qur'ân represent a wealth of ideas with various subtle shades of meaning that cannot be expressed in full with a single word equivalent in any language.

To illustrate, two Arabic terms from Al-Kahf (Chapter No. 18), namely *istâ`û* and *istatâ`û*, can be cited. Both terms are translated interchangeably as 'could' or 'was able to' by Sale, Muḥammad Ali, Pickthall, Rodwell, and others, all of whom overlooked the delicate difference in meaning between the two terms. The former is only used for relatively easy actions, such as climbing a wall, while the latter is used for harder tasks, such as making a hole in a solid wall. This is based on the Arabic rhetorical rule that the more letters a word has, the more or stronger meanings it denotes.

Another example can be the set of terms *mata* and *ayyân-a*, as the subtle difference between both have hardly been discerned in any translation the researcher has ever read. Though both stand for the interrogative 'when', the term *ayyân-a* implies a denial that the event in question will ever take place.

---

[80] Ayyoûb, *The awesome news,* xi.
[81] Bewley & Bewley, *The noble Qur'ân,* v.

Earlier, it was mentioned that a literal translation is neither possible nor acceptable. It also became clear that translating the implicit meanings of the Qur'ân, which mark its inimitability, goes beyond human capacity.

The basic meanings of the Qur'ân can be rendered into other languages. However, this also requires maximum caution so as not to charge these meanings with unintended associations. In fact, translators can only translate their own personal interpretation of the Qur'ân, or translate an authoritative interpretation prepared by a high-profile specialized committee. I accept the second option as it may reduce the vulnerability to err incurred by a single translator's personal understanding.

In this connection, it must be stressed that the inimitability of the Qur'ân does not prevent it from being translated, as there are various aspects of this inimitability. Some are 'Arabic-specific', as they are related to the language, style, and rhetoric of the Qur'ân, while others are 'general'. These general aspects can be realized by discerning people of different races.[82] These general aspects refer to: (a) the unseen; (b) narrations of the past; and (c) the legislations regulating various activities in life, be they private or public.

Hence, if the translation fails to convey the 'specific' aspect related to the style and rhetoric of the Qur'ân, it will not in any way affect the other aspects related to historic events and the like. It should also be borne in mind that the intended translation is of the meaning of the Qur'ân, not the Qur'ân itself, as was stated earlier.

Irving stated, "The Qur'an could be considered untranslatable, because each time one returns to the Arabic text, he finds new meanings and fresh ways of interpreting it."[83] Concerning the meaning, Irving warned that any

---

[82] Al-Lawindi, *Ishkaliyat Tarjamat Ma`ani Al-Qur'ân Al-Karim*, 29-30.

[83] Irving, *The Qur'ân: The first American version*, 27.

translation is affected by the translator's thoughts.[84] This is to say that Allah's Word could be manipulated in one way or another. To circumvent this, a methodical procedure is proposed in the Chapter titled: *How Should the Qur'ân Be Translated?*

---

[84] Ibid., 30.

8 PROBLEMS OF TRANSLATING THE QUR'ÂN

*"The Quran could be considered
untranslatable, because each time one
returns to the Arabic text, he finds new
meanings and fresh ways of interpreting it.
It is a living document."*

T. B. Irving (1985)

The need to translate the meanings of the Qur'ân coincided with the rise of Islam and its spread east and west. This occurred when non-Arabic speaking peoples reverted to Islam and, hence, needed to seek guidance from the Qur'ânic text.

In fact, the history of the translation of the Qur'ân is quite long and the list of translations is never ending as new translations appear constantly; even during the writing of these very lines, I received a new translation by a Jordanian translator. Running an exhaustive survey of all these translations or assessing them is not in any way among the purposes of this book, as this is far beyond its designed scope. Only a few translations will be touched upon for their significance and importance to many.

In 2001, Al-Lawindi attempted to numerate the translations of the Qur'ân into different world languages and found that there were up to 700 translations;[85] now, nearly 17 years later, you can imagine how many translations there are!

Principally, no single translation suffices any great work; "Every great book demands to be translated once in a century to suit the change in standards and taste of the new generations, which differ radically from those of the past."[86] The same view is held by Lefevere, who stated, "Different ages need different adjustments and translations."[87] Though tempted to agree with both scholars on this concept, the researcher objects to the duration they stated to produce a new rendition of such a great book as the Qur'ân. A span of 10 years is enough to warrant the production of a new rendition of the meaning of the Qur'ân to cope with the ever rapid rate of progress witnessed by our fast-moving world. Adding another difficulty as far as the translation of the Qur'ân is concerned, Irving emphasized, "The Quran could be considered untranslatable, because each time one returns to the Arabic text, he finds new meanings and fresh ways of interpreting it. It is a living document."[88] Thereupon, we have both external and internal requirements that demand a new translation as time changes.

A quick glance at the early translations of the Qur'ân shows that most of them contain distortions and refutations thereof. Even the titles of some were somehow biased and prejudiced. A German translation from 1772, for instance, is called 'The Turkish Bible'; the subtitle of another German rendition from 1616 reads (translated here in English),

---

[85] Al-Lawindi, *Ishkaliyat Tarjamat Ma`ani Al-Qur'ân Al-Karim.*

[86] Cohen, *English translators and translations,* 215.

[87] Lefevere, *Translating literature,* xi.

[88] Irving, *The Qur'ân: The first American version.*

"...from which one can learn about the origins of their false prophet Mohammed and to which occasion he has invented his fable and his ridiculous and foolish teachings."

In the 18th century, many translations of the Qur'ân were based on the then prevalent misconception that it was Prophet Muḥammad (peace be upon him) who authored the Qur'ân, and thus it was not the Word of God (Allah). Consequently, they considered the Qur'ân only as a historical document. Two major translations by Ross (1518) and Sale (1734) respectively were based on that false assumption. Of course, you can imagine the number and gravity of the mistakes made by translators based on this false allegation.

Early in the 20th century, some impartial Western translators emerged and their works were cordially received by many. These include Pickthall (1875-1936) and also Weiss (1900-1992), who reverted to Islam and changed his birth name to Muḥammad Asad.

It is to be stressed here that no translation of the Qur'ân is free from errors or mistakes, or can be deemed as a replacement for the Arabic Qur'ân in any way; this idea is very unacceptable. Even the more capable translators who were known for their honesty admitted that it is very hard and sometimes impossible to convey all the aesthetic aspects and eloquence of the Qur'ânic terms, concepts and style to any other language.

Unlike many previous translations that were made by individual translators, some were joint works carried out by two translators, such as that of Al-Hilali (1893-1987) and Khan (1927-...). Notably, a number of translations were authorized by official institutions, such as Al-Azhar and the Muslim World League, while many others did not receive such recognition or attention.

Translators' Common Mistakes

Recurrent and oft-repeated mistakes are usually made by

various translators of the Qur'ânic text for several reasons:

- The translator's prejudice may make him purposefully intend to misinterpret and even distort the meaning of the divine text of the Qur'ân; Ketton's (Latin: Robertus Ketenensis) (~1110-~1160) translation is a 'good' example of this.

- The translator's ignorance of the true meanings of the text may lead to him falling into many pitfalls. This can be traced back to either negligence or failure of comprehending what the books of *tafsîr* (Commentaries on the Qur'ân) say on the *ayahs* at hand. Both Muslim and non-Muslim, Arab and non-Arab translators alike may fall into this methodological mistake.

- The translator's competence may remain an obstacle in the path of producing a reliable translation of the Qur'ânic text. A translator may be aware of the true meanings of the text, but his capacity to reproduce it in the target language is below standard.

- The translator may tend not to differentiate between near synonyms with which the Arabic language in general and the Qur'ân in particular are replete. Thus, we find him using a single word to denote both *'shak'* and *'rayb'*, interchangeably translating them into English as either *'suspicion'* or *'doubt'*. The same is true of other near synonyms, such as *lawm*, *tathrîb* and *tafnîd*, as is mentioned in surah Yusuf. *Lawm*, *tathrîb* and *tafnîd* are all near synonyms denoting the meaning of reproaching or blaming someone for doing something bad. They only differ in the degree or intensity as they denote the strongest degree of blaming, a milder degree, and a much milder degree respectively.

- This takes us to another common mistake, which is the inconsistency in using English equivalents of the Arabic terms; a matter whose explanation goes beyond the scope of this book.

Finally, the translator may resort to adding explanatory notes which do not belong to the Qur'ânic text and have them embedded in a way that confuses the reader. A clear-cut way must be adopted to differentiate between the Qur'ânic text and any additional information the translator wishes to impart to the target reader. Actually, there are many acceptable methods to differentiate between the two!

ALI AL-HALAWANI

9 HOW SHOULD THE QUR'ÂN BE TRANSLATED?

*"Every great book demands to be translated
once in a century to suit the change in
standards and taste of the new
generations, which differ radically from
those of the past."*

J. M. Cohen (1962)

In order to obtain an accurate translation of the Qur'ân, the following should first be undertaken: A concise and clear-cut explanation of the Qur'ân should be prepared by a distinguished institution. This explanation should be so clear that translators can convey its meanings into other languages without needing to tackle the inimitable words of the Qur'ân or resorting to making their own interpretations. It is enough for the translator to undertake the difficult task of translation.

Preparation of such an explanation is not easy. It requires the joint efforts of a number of specialists in the fields of linguistics, translation studies, Islamic *sharî`ah*, Qur'ânic studies, and modes of the Qur'ânic recitation, along with experts in natural sciences, such as astronomy, biology, geology, medicine, etc. Most importantly, it should involve professional translators with a minimum experience of 20 years in the field of translating religious and Islamic texts. This is indispensable, for perfection cannot be achieved with poor tools. This committee should work under the auspices of either Al-Azhar (Egypt), King Fahd Quran Printing Complex (Saudi Arabia), the International Union for Muslim Scholars (IUMS), or a similar international body. Following the preparation of the interpretation of the Qur'ânic text by these specialists, the translation process commences. Only one or two translators are needed to actually translate the text after preparing the explanation; the rest of the translation team should then come aboard to meticulously read, review, verify, and demand necessary changes or modifications in a way that improves the work at hand. Eventually, a precise and authentic image of the Qur'ân may be reflected.

Simultaneously, another procedure should be carried out. That is, a second high-profile specialized committee should be formed to handle the already existing translations of the Qur'ân. The responsibilities of this committee should include, among other things: conducting a thorough examination of all the existing translations of the Qur'ân so as to; (a) approve the very few that are valid; (b) reject the bulk which are not up to standard; and (c) correct those which are amendable.

It is mandatory that the resolutions of such research and scholarly endeavors be published in notable periodicals in order to spread knowledge and benefit all those concerned: Muslim and non-Muslim researchers and translators, especially those who are interested in the translation of religious texts in general and the divine Qur'ânic text in particular.

Last but not less importantly, we should differentiate between the process of translation itself and the target behind this process. If the target was to convey the text of the Qur'ân in other languages, this could be carried out through one of three methods, as explained previously. However, if the target was to convey the meanings and the message of the Qur'ân using the best of all means that suit non-Arabic speaking Muslims and non-Muslims interested in the Qur'ân, the translation of a chosen explanation will be much more suitable and appropriate. This will serve the purposes of *da`wah* (propagation) and disseminating the message of the Qur'ân. In other words, and in view of the fact that non-Arabic speakers first need to understand what the Qur'ân says and not how it is said, it is better to translate the explanation and not the words of the Qur'ân.

The best way to conclude this section is to quote what Yusuf Ali stated in the introduction to his translation regarding the general meaning of the Qur'ân, highlighting the degree to which it is difficult to render into English the Islamic and *sharî`ah*-based terms that abound therein:

> "Every earnest and reverent student of the Qur'ân, as he proceeds with his study, will find with an inward joy difficult to describe, how this general meaning also enlarges as his own capacity for understanding increases. It is like a traveler climbing a mountain: the higher he goes the farther he sees. How much great[er] is the joy and sense of wonder and miracle when the Qur'ân opens our spiritual eyes! The meaning which we thought we had grasped extends... Such a meaning is most difficult to express."[89]

Nevertheless, the field remains open for future attempts to reflect the true meaning of the Qur'ân in another language, because this mandates not only an ability to produce a precise translation but also a better understanding of the text itself. It is becoming more and more apparent that the quest for the perfect rendition will be endless.

---

[89] Ali, *The holy Qur'ân: Text, translation and commentary*, v.

Golden rules for translating the Qur'ân

The following scheme is designed for the translation team to adopt upon seeking to render the Qur'ânic text into any TL. It is intended to help translators produce more precise and accurate renditions of the divine text. This scheme is based on a number of rules that were first introduced by Al-Maidâni in the context of teaching Muslims how to contemplate the Qur'ânic text to maximize their understanding thereof.[90] I believe these rules, with necessary changes, can be applied by translators in their pursuit of a precise translation of the Qur'ân into other languages. The modified rules read:

1. To consult Classical Arabic reference dictionaries on the various meanings and uses of the Qur'ânic term and/or expression at hand.

2. To define literal *vs.* figurative uses of the Qur'ânic term and/or expression as it was used by Arabs during the time the Qur'ân was being revealed.

3. To consider reported explanations from Prophet Muḥammad and take them as a frame for understanding Qur'ânic terms and/or expressions.

4. To study significant contributions of key commentators on the Qur'ân; this may give more enlightenment on the intended meaning.

5. To contemplate all occurrences of the term and/or expression in the Qur'ânic text; this may reveal the basic denotations as well as connotations of the term in the text at hand—whether it revolves around the lexical or the *sharî`ah*-based meaning, the literal or the figurative meaning, or both but in different contexts.

6. To recognize all relevant Islamic concepts side by side with other Qur'ânic concepts.

---

[90] Al-Maidâni, *Qawa`id al-Tadabbur al-Amthal li Kitab Allah*, 317-428.

7. To look thoroughly into the overall meaning of the text at hand while observing its context within the *surah*.

8. To determine the exact meaning of the term and/or expression at hand based on the aforementioned procedures; then to select the best possible equivalent thereof from the TL.

This TL equivalent should be able to communicate the 'obtained' exact meaning of the Qur'ânic term and/or expression without any trace of ambiguity or imprecision. There may even be an exact TL equivalent for the Arabic term and/or expression, so translators may think that they will not encounter any problems in transferring the meaning of such terms and/or expressions into the TL. However, they should be aware that the case is not that easy as far as the Qur'ân is concerned, as:

a. A Qur'ânic term may have a TL equivalent for one of its occurrences in the divine text, but require another equivalent (or more precisely, equivalents) for other occurrences, such as the term *'ummah'*, which can be rendered into English as 'a nation', 'a community', 'a group of people', 'a religion', 'a period', 'a time', 'a guide', etc., according to the context at hand.

b. The TL may have two variant equivalents or synonyms for a single Qur'ânic term and/or expression. Hence, the translator should choose the most suitable one in light of the Qur'ânic usage in the context at hand.

c. The TL may not have a perfect equivalent for the Qur'ânic term and/or expression. Hence, the translator should use the closest equivalent and support it with sufficient explanation that may appear in either a footnote or a glossary.

In preparing the explanation in the SL which will be transferred into TL, one should perfectly understand the meaning of the terms and/or expressions comprising the ST. Thus, understanding the Qur'ânic terms and expressions is of crucial importance to the success of the translation process *per se*. Therefore, consulting Classical Arabic dictionaries/lexicons is of major significance, particularly when there seems to be a contradiction between a scientific fact and the understanding of some commentators of particular *ayahs* in the Qur'ân. Let us consider the following Qur'ânic *ayah* which reads,

﴿وَٱلْأَرْضَ بَعْدَ ذَٰلِكَ دَحَىٰهَا﴾ and is translated into English as {And the earth, after this, He spread} (Al-Nazi`ât 79: 30).

Eight other different translations of the Qur'ân were consulted. It was found that the following English equivalents are used to denote the meaning of the term at hand: 'spread the earth', 'cast it', 'spread the earth', 'made the earth egg-shaped', 'spread out the earth', 'expanded it', 'spread forth', and 'extended (to a wide expanse)'. Clearly, all these equivalents revolve around two basic concepts, 'expansion' and 'making the earth egg-shaped'. Nevertheless, thorough examination of Classical Arabic lexicons may provide other possible interpretations which may be seen as more relevant to modern scientific discoveries.

Different classical commentators relied on the same concepts to denote the Arabic term *'daḫa'*. However, consulting Edward Lane's lexicon, an authentic rendition of Lisân Al-Arab by Ibn Manẕûr, proved the existence of other meanings and interpretations of the term that should have been considered upon explaining the meaning of the *ayah*. Indeed, expansion and spreading—adopted by almost all commentators—are among the meanings of the term. This can be justified as it represents the basic idea many people had regarding the flatness and relative levelness of the earth. However, other meanings, which are more relevant to recent astronomical discoveries, can be found therein. Hence, adding a significant dimension to the Qur'ân's scientific inimitability.

According to Edward Lane, '*daḫa*' stands for the following meanings 'He threw or cast...'. And, *yad-ḫu al-ḫijârata*, meaning...

> He threw, or cast, and impelled, propelled, or removed a stone from its place with his hand. One also says to him who is playing with walnuts, *ab'id-i al-mada wad-ḫi-hi*, meaning "Make thou the distance far, and throw it". And of rain, one says, *daḫa al-ḫasa 'an wajh-il arḍ-i*, meaning "It drove the pebbles from the surface of the earth; or removed them."[91]

He also said: *yad-ḫu al-ḫijârat-a*, meaning "to throw stones". *Al-madâḫ-i*, refers to stones, which are the shape of a small round cake called a *qurṣah*, and are thrown into a hole. This hole was dug to be the same size as these stones with the top edge of the hole (at the level of the ground) being slightly wider: if the stone falls therein, the person wins; but if not, he is overcome. You say of him *yad-ḫ-u*, when he throws the stones over the ground to the hole, and the hole is called *ad-ḫiyah*.[92]

These small stones roll or rotate around themselves while moving over the ground after being thrown. According to these Arabic uses of the term, *daḫa* implies two more concepts: (a) An act of throwing or pushing by the person involved; and (b) One of two movements witnessed by the thrown object, either to follow a specific course, or to rotate around its own axis. Considering the earth's movement, it resembles a huge rock 'thrown' in space with two movements: rotating around the sun and rotating around its own axis.

Accordingly, it is probable that the meaning of the *ayah* encompasses these kinds of movements side by side with the meaning of expansion and extension highlighted by all previous commentators.

---

91 Edward Lane, *An Arabic-English lexicon*, 857.
92 Ibid.

As was mentioned earlier, this scheme can be applied by high-profile specialized committees or translation teams undertaking the task of translating the Qur'ânic text. But if an explanation of the Qur'ân cannot be prepared by specialized committees under the auspices of any distinguished body, the scheme can also be applied by individuals or a group of translators. Preparation of such a translation is not easy.

10 SELECTED TRANSLATIONS OF THE QUR'ÂN

*"The Muslim Scripture is yet to find a dignified
and faithful expression in the English language
that matches the majesty and grandeur of the
original. The currents of history, however, seem
to be in favour of such a development. Even
English is acquiring a native Muslim character
and it is only a matter of time before we have a
worthy translation of the Qur'ân in that tongue."*

A. R. Kidwai (1987)

Here, a number of translations of the meanings of the Qur'ân will be introduced for their significance and the fame they have gained in many countries in the present day. This is based completely on my personal judgment, which can be either supported or objected to by others.

I have chosen these translations for a number of reasons; foremost among which are what follows:

1. They were undertaken directly from the Arabic source text; i.e. the Arabic Qur'ân itself.

2. They were not based on previous translations under the pretext of improving or correcting the previous ones.

3. They are quite famous and known to many, as was just mentioned.

4. They were based on the mode of recitation of Ḥafṣ from ʿAṣim, and do not take account of other modes in order not to confuse the reader.

5. They guarantee the representation of various cultural and educational backgrounds as far as the translators are concerned.

Details of these translations and their translators are given below to present them in their proper historical and subjective context.

1. Muḥammad Marmaduke Pickthall (1875-1936)

Pickthall was an English man of letters whose literary and historical works were published in distinguished magazines in London and New York. His translation is titled, *The Meaning of the Glorious Qur'ân*, and it was first published in 1930. It is regarded as one of the most widely used translations all over the world.

Many specialists in translating the meanings of the Qur'ân have agreed that there is no translation better than Pickthall's in terms of the beauty of its style, eloquence and adherence to the Sunni Muslim creed. It is so carefully worded that it corresponds perfectly with the Arabic text; a matter that keeps it meticulously close to the original in elegant English. However, the English he used is now somewhat archaic and thus tends to be an obstacle for a nonprofessional who wishes to read his translation.

He made his translation directly from the Arabic without any intermediation. In Pickthall's view, the Qur'ân cannot be translated and his work was nothing but a mere attempt to present the meanings of the Qur'ân into English. He faithfully tried to represent the sense of the original, and thus his rendition was almost literal. He did not exert himself to make his notes helpful for the reader of his translation as they lacked sufficient information on the circumstantial setting of the *surahs* and the subtle meanings of the Qur'ânic text.

2. Abdullah Yusuf Ali (1872-1953)

Ali was a Muslim scholar who had an excellent command of both Arabic and English. He was principal of the Islamic College, Lahore. His translation was first published under the title, *The Holy Qur'ân: Translation and Commentary*, 1934-37. It is perhaps the most popular achievement in the field, as it stands out above many other translations due to the elegant style in which it was written along with the chaste English that composed its sentences and phrases.

Ali's rendering of the Qur'ânic *ayahs* is in blank verse which, according to him, is more suitable for conveying something of the Qur'ân's inimitable symphony to its readers. The requirements of prosody, however, made it inevitable that he alter the word order of the original Arabic text. He has also occasionally deviated from a literal rendering.

Unlike Pickthall, Ali adds some valuable comments at the bottom of each page to help the reader comprehend the text correctly. His prolific notes are reflective of his vast knowledge. Nonetheless, some of these notes, particularly on the Hereafter and details about the unseen, tend to be apologetic and pseudo-rationalist. His bias towards Sufism is also quite marked in his notes.

3. Arthur John Arberry (1905–1969)

Arberry was a renowned Orientalist and professor of Arabic at the universities of London and Cambridge. He was also head of the Department of Classics at Cairo University in Egypt.

He first published his translation under the title, *The Koran Interpreted*, 1955, by Oxford University Press. No doubt, Arberry's translation stands out above other English translations ever undertaken by non-Muslims in terms of both its approach and quality. Nonetheless, it is not altogether free from mistakes as it has, at certain places, faults such as omissions and mistranslations. Like the former two translators, Arberry made his translation directly from the Arabic, which is an important criterion, as stated earlier.

Despite the fact that Arberry was a non-Arab and a non-Muslim, he had moderate views about Islam and the Qur'ân. He was of the opinion that the Qur'ân is too great to be translated; hence, he chose to name his work 'an interpretation' rather than 'a translation', which he deemed beyond human capacity as far as the Qur'ân is concerned.

On the other hand, he disagreed with Reverend Rodwell who rendered the Qur'ân under the title, *The Koran: Translation from the Arabic*, 1861, on many of his views, especially the belief that the Qur'ân is not the word of God (Allah) revealed to Muhammad (peace be upon him).

Citing a contemporary translator of the Qur'ân commenting on Arberry's rendering, Abdel Haleem writes,

> "Arberry shows great respect towards the language of the Qur'ân, particularly its musical effects. His careful observation of Arabic sentence structure and phraseology makes his translation very close to the Arabic original in grammatical terms ... [however] this feature, along with the lack of any notes or comments, can make the text seem difficult to understand

and confusingly unidiomatic."[93]

The Koran Interpreted was originally published in two volumes, the first containing surahs 1-20, the second containing surahs 21-114. The text is still printed nowadays, normally in one volume.

4. Muḥammad Taqi-ud-Din Al-Hilali (1893-1987) & Muḥammad Muḥsin Khan (1927-...)

This translation is called, *The Noble Qur'ân*, and is also informally known as *The Hilali-Khan translation*. It was first published in 1977. It is a translation of the Qur'ân by contemporary Afghani Islamic scholars Muḥammad Muḥsin Khan (b. 1927) and Muḥammad Taqui Al-Din Al-Hilali (1893-1987).

Al-Hilali taught at universities in England, Baghdad and Madinah. Khan was born in the Punjab Province in Pakistan, his family having emigrated earlier from Afghanistan. He studied medicine at the universities of Punjab and Wales. He worked as a medical doctor, a Minister of Health in Saudi Arabia, and later a department director at Kings Hospital and after that Al-Madinah University Clinic in Al-Madinah Al-Munawwarah, Saudi Arabia.

Both translators have been introduced as being *Salafi* (i.e. traditional followers of the way of the Prophet and the early Muslims). The translation is intended to present the meanings of the Qur'ân which the early Muslims had understood.

The scholars translated from the original Arabic source text. It is heavily interspersed with commentaries and explanatory notes from Al-Ṭabari (d. 224-310 AH), Al-Qurṭubi (d. 671 AH) and Ibn Kathîr (700-774 AH), to the extent that it could be called a summarized version of all these commentaries on the Qur'ân, along with comments from Imam Bukhari's collection of authentic hadîth, Ṣaḥîḥ Al-

---

[93] Abdel Ḥaleem, *The Qur'an, a new translation*, xxviii.

Bukhari (194-256 AH).

However, many have criticized their translation because these notes abound throughout the translated text, and to some, it was even "more like a supremacist Muslim, anti-Semitic, anti-Christian polemic than a rendition of the Islamic scripture."[94] Moreover, Musaji complained that it is "shocking in its distortions of the message of the Qur'ân and amounts to a rewrite, not a translation."[95] In addition, Ghali criticized the existence of the 'human element', as he calls it, in the translation. He regards this work something other than a translation because of the abundance in terms of footnotes and commentaries that interrupt the original text. He also wonders about the authenticity of the ḥadîths added to the text, whether they are all authentic or not.[96]

Still, I decided to include this translation here because it is one of the very few that was carried out as a joint effort because it was handled by two translators. Moreover, despite all these criticisms, it is still held in high esteem by a wide range of *Salafi* Muslims—a matter which cannot be ignored. In addition, it greatly helps in promoting Islamic and *sharî`ah*-based terminology in a manner that paves the way for creating the desired Islamic English, as was called for by the late Al-Faruqi (1921-1986 AC). It does so by using Arabic terms in transliterated form followed by a partial equivalent English term.

5. Muḥammad Maḥmoud Ghali (1920-2016)

Ghali was one of the leading international figures in the field of Islamic studies in general and in translating the meanings of the Qur'ân in particular. Ghali obtained his PhD

---

[94] Khaleel, *Assessing English translations of the Qur'ân*, 58-71.

[95] Musaji, *Through the looking glass: Hilali-Khan Qur'an Translation*, www.theamericanmuslim.org.

[96] Ghali, *On the translation of the meanings of the ever-glorious Qur'ân*, www.IslamOnline.net.

in Phonetics from the University of Michigan. He also studied Phonetics at the University of Exeter in the UK. He is the founder of the Faculty of Languages and Translation, Al-Azhar University. Besides teaching in the university, he was also a permanent member of many Islamic organizations in Egypt, Saudi Arabia, Turkey, and other countries working in the field of translating the meanings of the Qur'ân into different languages.

Ghali spent around 20 years working on his translation of the meanings of the Qur'ân. His translation is published under the title, *Towards Understanding the Ever-Glorious Qur'ân,* and is regarded by many as a masterpiece.

Of all the translations made into English, none had, until recently, been made by scholars whose native language was Arabic. At present, however, three such translations have been made, one by Ghali, another by Ahmed and Dina Zidan, and a third by Abdel Haleem, who is also an Egyptian.

Ghali's translation clearly shows that the translator has gone to the trouble of consulting the well-known Arabic commentaries; a matter which resulted in a translation which has all the appearance of accuracy.

Ghali endeavored to revise most of the translations of the meanings of the Qur'ân into English: around twenty translations that were issued over the last decades in different parts of the world. He also presented detailed scholarly reports on these translations to the concerned Islamic bodies and organizations. Among the translations he revised were that of Zidan which was released in Britain in 1999. Another translation he revised was that of *The Select* by Abu Shabanah, released by the Supreme Council for Islamic Affairs, Egypt, as well as many others.

He also laid the foundations of an integrated theory for translating the meanings of the Qur'ân to languages other than Arabic. This can be explained in three points as follows:

1. Only the Qur'ânic text should be translated and not
    the commentary on the text, as conveying the words'
    meanings should be the main concern of the
    translator rather than anyone's personal interpretation
    of these words. He further considers it forbidden to
    introduce the translation of a commentary as if it
    were a translation of the Qur'ân itself. This is
    because, according to him, it constitutes two-degrees
    of separation from the Qur'ân itself: one degree for
    the commentary and another for the translation. In
    addition, the translation of a commentary represents
    a translation of the thoughts of the commentator
    himself and his own method of interpreting the
    Qur'ân, which is prone to error.

2. He meticulously distinguishes between synonyms
    applying the theory stating that each term in the
    Qur'ân is intended by itself and it does not typically
    match with its synonymous terms, regardless of the
    similarities. This corresponds well with the comments
    of Ibn `Attiyah that were mentioned earlier.

3. He admits that no translation is error-free and, hence,
    all translations require constant revision—a matter
    which conforms to the regeneration of the meanings
    of the Qur'ân and its dynamic nature. This is also in
    conformity with the semantic change that is
    widespread in languages other than Arabic.

Finally, the field remains open for future attempts to
reflect the true meaning of the Qur'ân, because this mandates
not only translation but also a better understanding of its text
and context alike. Truly, the quest for a 'perfect' rendition of
the divine text seems endless.

BIBLIOGRAPHY

`Itir, N. (1992). *Al-Qur'ân al-karim wal dirasat al-adabiyah* [The glorious Qur'ân and the literary studies]. Syria: Damascus University.

Abdel Haleem, M. A. S. (2004). *The Qur'ân, a new translation*. New York: Oxford University Press.

Abdullah, M. J. (1998). *`Azamat al-Qur'ân wa da`watihi ila al-khair wal kamal* [Greatness of the Qur'ân and its call for goodness and perfection]. Egypt: Al-Nuzha Bookstore.

Abdul-Raof, H̱. (2001). *Quran translation: Discourse, texture and exegesis*. Leeds, U.K.: Curzon Press.

Abu Laylah, M. M. (1997). *The Qur'ân and the gospels: A comparative study*. Cairo: El-Falah for Translation, Publishing & Distribution.

Al-Alaya'a, Z. (2005). *The Arabic language, the root of all languages*. Yemen Observer, Sep. 10. www.mafhoum.com [Accessed 9th June 2008].

Al-Aqqad, A. M. (n.d.). *Al-lughah al-sha`irah* [The poetic language]. Cairo: Maktabat Gharib.

Al-Baqillani, A. B. (1954). *I`jaz al-Qur'ân* [Inimitability of the

Qur'ân]. (Ed.) Al-Sayyid Ahmad Saqr. Cairo: Dar Al-Ma`arif.

Al-Baquri, A. H. (1987). *Athar al-Qur'ân al-karim fi al-lughah al-`arabiyah* [Impact of the glorious Qur'ân on the Arabic language]. Cairo: Dar Al-Ma`arif.

Al-Faruqi, I. R. (1986). *Toward Islamic English* (No. 3). International Institute of Islamic Thought (IIIT).

Al-Ghazzali, A. H. (1988). *Jawahir al-Qur'ân wa duraruh* [Jewels and pearls of the Qur'ân]. Lebanon: Dar Al-Jil & Dar Al-Afaq Al-Jadidah.

Al-Halawani, A. (2016). Eight-point scheme proposal for translating the Qur'ânic text. *US-China Education Review A*, *6*(2), 91-104.

Al-Hilali, T., & Khan, M. (1977). *Explanatory English translation of the holy Qur'ân: A summarized version of ibn Kathir supplemented by Al-Tabari with comments from sahih al-Bukhari*. Riyadh: Dar Al-Salam.

Ali, A. Y. (1973). *The Holy Qur'ân: text, translation and commentary*. Saudi Arabia: Islamic University of Al imam Mohammad ibn SA'UD.

Al-Jabari, R. (2008). *Reasons for the possible incomprehensibility of some verses of three translations of the meaning of the holy Quran into English* (Ph.D. dissertation, School of Languages, University of Salford, Salford, UK).

Al-Jahiz, A. U. A. (1965). *Al-Hayawan* [The animal]. Cairo: Al-Halabî Press.

Al-Jindi, A. (1982). *Al-fus-ha: Lughat al-Qur'ân* [Classical standard Arabic is the language of the Qur'ân]. Lebanon: Dar al-Kitab al-Lubnani.

Al-Jurjani, A. M. (1995). *Al-ta`rifat* [The definitions]. (Ed.) Abdel Mun`im Al-Hifni. Egypt: Dar al-Rashad.

Al-Lawindi, S. (2001). *Ishkaliyat tarjamat ma`ani al-Qur'ân al-karim* [Problem of translating the meanings of the glorious Qur'ân]. Cairo: Markaz al-Ḥaḍarah al-Arabiyah.

Al-Maidani, A. R. Ḥ. (2004). *Qawa`id al-tadabbur al-amthal li kitab Allah* [Rules for the best contemplation over the book of Allah]. Damascus: Dar al-Qalam.

Al-Makhzumî, M., & Al-Samirâeî, I. (Eds.). (1988). *Al-`Ain* [The eye]. Lebanon, Beirut: Al-A`lamî Foundation for Printing.

Al-Nawawi, Sh. A. (1987). *Al-tibyan fi adab ḥamalat al-Qur'ân* [The clarification on the etiquettes of memorizers of the Qur'ân]. Lebanon: Dar Al-Nafa'is.

Al-Qaṭṭan, M. Kh. (1990). *Mabaḥith fi `ulum al-Qur'ân* [Studies in Qur'ânic sciences]. Cairo: Wahbah Publishing House.

Al-Qur'ân Al-Karîm [The glorious Qur'ân]. (2009). Ministry of Endowments and Islamic Affairs, Qatar. Turkey, Istanbul: Mas Printing House.

Al-Rafi`i, M. S. (1997). *I`jaz al-Qur'ân wal-balaghah al-nabawiyyah* [Inimitability of the Qur'ân and the prophetic rhetoric]. Cairo: Al-Maktabah Al-Tawfiqiyah.

Al-Shabab, O. S. (1998). *Translating with difference: Theory and practice.* Damascus, Syria: DEBS.

Al-Shaṭibi, A. I. (2003). *Al-muwafaqat fi usul al-shari`ah* [Agreements on the fundamentals of shari`ah]. Commentary by Abdullah Draz. Cairo: Al-Tawfikia Bookshop.

Al-Sulaiti, L., & Atwell, E. (2004). *Designing and developing a corpus of contemporary Arabic* (Doctoral dissertation, University of Leeds (School of Computing)).

Al-Suyuti, A. R. J. A. (1987). *Al-muzhir fi ulum al-lughah wa anwa`iha,* [Al-muzhir in the sciences of language and its types]. (Ed.) Abul Faḍl Ibrahim and others. Lebanon: Al-Maktabah al-Aṣryyiah.

Al-Suyuti, A. R. J. A. (2004). *Al-itqan fi `ulum al-Qur'ân* [Perfection in the sciences of the Qur'ân]. (Ed.) Aḥmad

Ibn Ali. Cairo: Dar Al-Ḥadith.

Al-Zamakhshari, A. Q. (1998). *Al-kashshaf* [The explorer]. (Ed.) Adel Abdel Mawjud & Ali Mu`awwad. Saudi Arabia: Obeikan Publishers.

Al-Zurqani, M. A. A. (2004). *Manahil al-`irfan* [Fountains of gratitude]. Lebanon: Dar Al-Fikr.

Arberry, A. J. (1955). trans. *The Koran Interpreted*. Macmillan.

Arberry, A. J. (2008). *The holy Koran: An introduction with selections*. New York, N.Y.: Routledge/Taylor & Francis Group.

Arbuthnot, F. F. (1985). *The construction of the Bible and the Koran*. London, U.K.: Watts.

Ayoub, M. (1997). *The awesome news*. Hiawatha, Iowa: Cedar Graphics.

Barakah, A. Gh. M. (1989). *Al-i`jaz al-Qur'âni: wujuhihi wa asrarih* [Inimitability of the Qur'ân: aspects and secrets]. Cairo: Wahbah Publishing House.

Bewley, A., & Bewley, A. (2005). *The noble Qur'ân: A new rendering of its meanings in English*. Norwich: Bookwork.

Catford, J. C. (1965). *A linguistic theory of translation*. Oxford: Oxford University Press.

Cohen, J. M. (1962). *English translators and translations* (No. 142). British Council.

Daimi, K. (2001). Identifying syntactic ambiguities in single-parse Arabic sentence. *Computers and the Humanities, 35*(3), 333-349.

Daimi, K., & Abdel-Amir, M. (1994). The syntactic analysis of Arabic by machine. *Computers and the Humanities, 28*(1), 29-37.

Daryabadi, A. M. (2002). *The glorious Qur'ân: Text, translation & commentary (Koran)*. U.K.: The Islamic Foundation.

Denffer, A. V. (2009). *Ulum Al-Quran: An introduction to the sciences of the Quran*. Leicester, U.K.: The Islamic Foundation.

Dickins, J., Hervey, S. G. J., & Higgins, I. (2002). *Thinking Arabic translation, a course in translation method: Arabic to English*. Abingdon, U.K.: Routledge.

Eliwa, A. H̱. (2004). *Synonymy and Lexical Collocation in Classical Arabic: A Corpus-based Study*. Unpublished Thesis. England: University of Manchester.

Ghali, M. M. (1998). *Towards understanding the ever-glorious Qur'ân*. Cairo: Publishing House for Universities.

Ghali, M. M. (1998b). *Tafsir al-Qur'ân al-karim bil al-sinah al-ajnabiyah* [Interpreting the ever-glorious Qur'ân into foreign languages]. In *Proceedings of the International Conference on Translation and Its Role in Civilizations Interaction*. Egypt: Al-Azhar University.

Ghali, M. M. (1998c). *A'imat al-nuḫah* [Leaders of grammarians]. Egypt: Publishing House for Universities.

Ghali, M. M. (2004). *On the Translation of the Meanings of the Ever-Glorious Qur'ân*. An Internet-radio interview. www.IslamOnline.net, October 26 [Accessed 20th July 2007].

Ghunaim, K. A. (1990). *Al-lughah al-`arabiyyah wal saḫwah al-`ilmiyyah al-ḫadithah*, [The Arabic language and the modern scientific awakening]. Egypt: Ibn Sina Bookstore.

Guillaume, A. (1949). *The legacy of Islam*. Oxford, U.K.: Oxford University Press.

Haeri, N. (2003). *Sacred language, ordinary people: Dilemmas of culture and politics in Egypt*. New York, N.Y.: Palgrave Macmillan.

Hammâd, A. Z. (2009). *The gracious Qur'ân*. USA: Lucent Interpretations, LLC.

Hilali-Khan Qur'an Translation. The American Muslim Website: www.theamericanmuslim.org. Posted Feb. 1, 2006. Last logged in June 17, 2016.

Hitti, P. K. (1958). *History of the Arabs*. New York, N.Y.: Macmillan.

Hussein, T. (1948). *Hadith al-shi`r wal nathr* [Discussion on poetry and prose]. Cairo: Dar Al-Ma`arif.

Ibn Faris, A. (1997). *al-sahibi fi fiqh al-lughah al-`arabiyyah* [The comrade in Arabic philology]. (Ed.) Ahmad Hassan Basag. Lebanon: Dar al-Kutub al-`Ilmiyyah.

Irving, T. B. (1993). *The Qur'an: the noble reading*. Mother Mosque Foundation.

Khaleel, M. (2005). Assessing English translations of the Qur'ân. *Middle East Quarterly, 12*(2), 58-71.

Khoja, S. (2003). A tagset for the morphosyntactic tagging of Arabic. *A Rainbow of Corpora: Corpus Linguistics and the Languages of the World*.

Lane (1980). *An Arabic-English lexicon*. Lebanon: Libraire Du Liban.

Lane, E. W. (1879). *Selections from the Kur-an* (Vol. 30). Houghton, Osgood, & Company.

Lefevere, A. (1977). *Translating literature: the German tradition from Luther to Rosenzweig* (No. 4). Rodopi.

Levy, J. (1967). Translation as a decision process. In *To honour Roman Jakobson: Essays on the occasion of his seventieth birthday* (October 11, 1966, Vol. 2.). The Hague: Mouton.

Muir, W. (1894). *Life of Mohamet* (Vol. 1). London.

Musaji, S. (2006). *Through the looking glass: Hilali-Khan Qur'an translation*. The American Muslim Website: www.theamericanmuslim.org. Posted Feb. 1, 2006 [Accessed 17 June 2008].

Musallam, M. (1999). *Mabahith fi i`jaz al-Qur'ân* [Studies on the inimitability of the Qur'ân]. Damascus: Dar Al-Qalam.

Noack, R., & Gamio, L. (2015). The world's languages, in 7 maps and charts. Retrieved September 22, 2015, from http://www.washingtonpost.com/news/worldviews/wp/2015/04/23/the-worlds-languages-in-7-maps-and-charts/

O'Donnell, M. B. (2004). Translation and the exegetical process, using marks 5.1-10: "The binding of the strong man", as a test case. In S. E., Porter, & R. S., Hess (Eds.), *Translating the Bible: Problems and prospects*. T & T Clark International, A Continuum imprint.

Pickthall, M. M. W. (1930). *The meaning of the glorious Qur'ân*. Hyderabad-Deccan: Government Central Press.

Potter, C. F. (1959). *The faiths men live by*. The World's Work (1913) Ltd., Kingswood, Surrey.

Salama-Carr, M. (2011). Interpretive Approach. In Baker, M & Saldanha, G (ed.) Routledge Encyclopaedia of Translation Studies. 2nd edition, Routledge.

Shahin, A. A. (1986). *Al-`arabiyyah lughat al-`ulum wal taqniyyah* [Arabic is the language of sciences and technology]. Cairo: Dar al-I`tisam.

Tibawi, A. L. (1962). Is the translation of the Qur'ân possible? Early Muslim opinions. *The Muslim World, 52*, 17-28.

Versteegh, K. (1991). Greek translations of the Quran in Christian polemics (Ninth Century A.D). *Zeitschrift der Deutschen Morgenlandischen Gesellschaft, 141*(1), 52-68.

Wherry, E. M. (2006). *A comprehensive commentary on the Qur'ân*. Whitefish, M. T.: Kessinger Publishing, LLC.

Zaqzuq, M. H. (Ed.) (2006). *Al-mawsu`ah al-Qur'âniyah al-mutakhasisah* [The specialized Qur'ânic encyclopedia]. Cairo: The Supreme Council of Islamic Affairs.

OTHER BOOKS BY THE AUTHOR

He authored the following books:

1. *Translation of Collocations in the Qur'an.* Malaysia: IIUM Press.

2. *Lasting Solutions to Social Problems.* (In print)

His translations from English into Arabic and vice versa include the following books:

1. Bulac, A. *Turkey's Democracy Saga: The Struggle Against Interventionist Politics.* New Jersey: Blue Dome Press.

2. Bozkurt, A. *Turkey Interrupted: Derailing Democracy.* New Jersey: Blue Dome Press.

3. Onat, S. *Islamic Art of Illumination: Classical Tazhib from Ottoman to Contemporary Times.* New Jersey: Blue Dome Press.

4. Kuşoğlu, M. Z. *Silver in Turkish Art.* New Jersey: Blue Dome Press.

5. Kuşoğlu, M. Z. *The Ottoman Touch: Traditional Decorative Arts and Crafts.* New Jersey: Blue Dome Press.

6. Al-Sheikh, A. R. *Divine Triumph: Explanatory Notes on the Book of Tawhid.* Egypt: El-Manarah Publishing House.

7. Ibn Kathir. *Stories of the Qur'ân.* Egypt: El-Manarah Publishing House.

8. Al-Hakami, H. *200 FAQs on Muslim Belief.* Egypt: El-Manarah Publishing House.

He also co-translated the following books:

1. Al-Qaradawi, Y. *The State in Islam.* Egypt: El-Falah Foundation.

2. Mahmoud, A. A. *Methods of Education.* Egypt: Dar Al-Tawzi` wal Nashr

3. Ayyoub, H. *Fiqh for the Muslim Family.* Egypt: El-Falah Foundation.

4. Abdul Hadi, J. *Islam: The Religion of Allah.* Egypt: El-Falah Foundation.

5. Al-Tahhan, M. *How to Attain a Perfect Muslim Character in the Modern World.* Egypt: El-Falah Foundation.